Are you one of those people who wish
the thought of opening your home s
don't have a big enough home or you a
freaked out by reaching out and invit
weird? What if they say no?")

I get it . . . because that's been me so many times too! And that's why
Jen's book left me crazy convicted and inspired. In her down-to-earth style,
she gives you the inspiration and motivation you need to baby step out of
your comfort zone and get brave enough to open the door to your home and
your heart—no matter the size of your home or your budget!

Crystal Paine, founder of MoneySavingMom.com and
New York Times best-selling author of *Say Goodbye to Survival Mode*

What I love most about this book is that, in addition to countless creative
ideas and wonderful hospitality tips, Jen gives us a bigger perspective of
what it means to live a life of welcome! Instead of feeling guilty because I
don't invite people over as much as I want to, *Just Open the Door* gave me
hope by showing me how to live a life of hospitality on the go. I'm so grateful for this gift of grace that has helped me see hospitality is about making
a difference right where we are with what we already have!

Renee Swope, best-selling author of *A Confident Heart*
and former radio cohost, Proverbs 31 Ministries

If the mere mention of hostessing makes you want to pull your blinds, lock
the door, or dive under the table, don't panic. *Just Open the Door* offers an
unexpected but encouraging invitation for all of us.

With humor and grace, stories, and solid scripture, Jen gently reshapes
what we think hospitality has to look like and opens the door to consider
what radical biblical hospitality feels like.

Jen invites us into this conversation just as we are (bedlam and all),
but I guarantee if we take the message to heart, we won't stay the same. *Just
Open the Door* is a gift that will leave you refreshed, challenged, and inspired
to live a life of welcome and worship in your home and neighborhood!

Melissa Michaels, creator of *The Inspired Room* blog,
New York Times best-selling author of *Love the Home You Have,*
Make Room for What You Love, and *Simple Gatherings*

There's no one I'd rather follow through the door of hospitality than my
dear friend Jen Schmidt. Come open your heart to her message of God's
grace and His goodness. Soak up these pages and learn from our lovable
teacher that the practice of hospitality does not have to be a burden. There

is more rest and joy waiting than we have known. Just open this book and let your soul receive its wisdom. Let your heart laugh and be light. Let your life be stirred to love others more like Christ has already loved us.

Angela Thomas Pharr, Bible teacher and best-selling author
of *Redeemed: Grace to Live Every Day Better Than Before*

Finally, a hospitality book for all of us "good enough is good enough" gals! Jen is everyone's big sister when it comes to giving us the much-needed nudge to quit sweating the décor and just start opening the door. Whether that ends up looking like potluck on paper plates or fine dining by candlelight, her focus is always on the people more than the place settings, and that's what's made all the difference in my own real-life, everyday invitations!

Lisa-Jo Baker, best-selling author of
Never Unfriended and *Surprised by Motherhood*

Through her blog, her conference, and her friendship, Jen has always inspired me to be more intentional about parenting and running my home without feeling like it all needs to be perfect. Equal parts encouragement and motivation, *Just Open the Door* makes us realize that being hospitable doesn't have to be complicated.

Ruth Soukup, *New York Times* best-selling author
of *Living Well, Spending Less: 12 Secrets of the Good Life* and
Unstuffed: Decluttering Your Home, Mind, and Soul

Full of grace, relatability, and permission, Jen's message of encouragement is one every reluctant hostess longs to hear. For anyone who continues to put off having people over until next time, *Just Open the Door* is your new mantra.

Myquillyn Smith, "The Nester," author of
The Nesting Place and *The Cozy Minimalist Home*

This wonderful book will redefine what hospitality truly is. Jen brilliantly shows that it isn't limited to large groups and big parties but can also be one-on-one interaction, coffee and heartfelt conversation with a dear friend.

Just Open the Door is a gift. It will help you finally break away from the bondage of self-doubt and excuses to become the hostess you've always dreamed of being!

Christy Jordan, publisher of SouthernPlate.com,
best-selling cookbook author, and TV personality

Just Open
the Door

Just Open *the* Door

How **One** Invitation **Can Change** a Generation

(in)courage author
JEN SCHMIDT

B&H
PUBLISHING GROUP
NASHVILLE, TENNESSEE

Because of my mom and dad, who first opened the door to me.

To Gregg, my husband, my love, the faithful
servant who makes this house a home.

In honor of my sweet blessings: Taylor, Matthew, David,
Abby, and Emma. May you continue this legacy of open-door
living and point others to Him. You are my next chapter.

Contents

In the Beginning, Just Start

As I think back on where my legacy of hospitality started, my memories surround our childhood doorway.

I can't really describe it in great detail. That's how little its appearance even mattered. But I do remember its purpose. It housed both a storm door and a screen door. The heavy door kept out the brutal Wisconsin winter, while the other door contained a large screen for those rare days when we captured the magic of spring and summer.

My favorite days growing up? The ones when that screen door announced action.

Slam. In.

Slam. Out.

I'd hear it again. Slam. Slam.

"In or out?" my mom's voice echoed through the house. "Please stop slamming the door." To me, though, that slam was never one of annoyance. Its recurring sound breathed life. It meant things were happening.

Dropping their mud-covered bikes on our grass, kids stormed through the door hoping my brothers could play.

Slam.

A neighbor lady popped her head in, asking for an extra egg.

Slam.

A missionary family, spending the week with us while home on furlough, returned from an errand or a nearby speaking engagement.

Slam. Slam.

But more than anything, I remember hearing the sound of that door on Sunday nights.

Slam. Slam. Slam.

Long before *Field of Dreams* popularized the phrase, my parents had already personified the message of "If you build it, they will come." With a genuine love for others, and inspired by an outsized vision for impacting their community, they defied the indoor space limitations of our fifteen-hundred-square-foot house and poured a concrete pad in the backyard. Thus began an informal volleyball league, meeting every Sunday night. Friends, kids, and strangers alike gathered from all over. Simple snacks lined the table, complete with stacks of coolers filled with cold drinks. Smoky aromas from a charcoal grill wafted through the air. Laughter mingled with the casual delights of shared conversation, punctuated by roars of cheering and applause for points scored and exceptional plays. High-fives all around.

Slam. Slam. Slam. Slam. Slam.

There was never anything fancy about it. "Come Sunday night, bring your favorite beverage, a little something to eat, and let's have fun playing together." But I'm telling you, a whole lot more than volleyball took place on those incredibly memorable evenings of my childhood. What started out as a loosely connected community came together around a game, only to turn into friendships that lingered into lasting relationships. Life after life. Story after story.

I was there. I saw it. I heard it. My parents—an ordinary couple—made a deliberate decision, intent on getting to know the people around them from more than a polite distance. I didn't even realize they were modeling anything special. They were simply living the natural outflow of their faith, putting a smiling face on their heart of welcome. But the aroma it created drew others in. And it wasn't just the aroma of Wisconsin brats roasting on an open fire. It was so much more.

It changed the dynamic. It changed people's lives.

Because hospitality has the power to change a generation.

I know I'm issuing a bold declaration with these words—"change a generation"—but I don't offer it lightly. I genuinely believe we can change a generation with something as simple as an invitation.

And I say, why not yours? I've sure seen it change mine.

The stories you're about to read, the ideas you're about to glean—none of them started with me. But from my front-row seat, observing what started with my parents, I've witnessed three generations of families continuing to extend these simple invitations. And as a result of God working through such heart-to-heart interactions, I've seen friendships formed, relationships restored, outsiders welcomed, and the gospel come to life. Together these experiences excite me as some of my favorite, most memorable chapters, with many other chapters yet to be written, still in process. I don't know how it's all going to turn out—it's a cliff-hanger, so to speak—but it's sure to be amazing. Rich in faith, in goodness, in fun, and in deep, deep meaning.

And nothing would mean more to me than for you to come along . . . to write your own ending while I'm here writing mine.

Life is always better with another. So, can we walk this road of welcome together? Begin where we are? And just start? I'm doing the writing, I know—complete with sweaty palms and a nervous tummy, terrified my words won't communicate the sense of urgency I feel. But I'm asking you to accept the invitation because this message matters. It's transformative. It's the start of a legacy. It can reshape things to come.

As we go along, each chapter will touch on a highly relatable area of life, one in which opening your door can meet with varying levels of challenge and discomfort, but also with unexpected opportunity and incredible new depths of relationship. But that's not all we'll do together. For additional fun and insight, I've included a number of "Dear Jen" letters I've received through the years, answered by a few words of understanding advice. You'll see you're not the only one asking the same kinds of questions. And I sure don't mind helping you learn from some of my own mistakes! Plus, to help surround your good intentions with truly workable suggestions, I end each chapter with all kinds of proven, practical ideas to help you "Elevate the Ordinary"—things I've tried myself or seen others do to make opening our doors easy, effective, and naturally inviting. Put these tips together with your own prayer and creativity, and who knows what God might inspire you to do!

Oh, and—like I said—since I've seen up-close the profound generational impact of families who are absolutely devoted to Christian hospitality, and because I want the same so dearly for you, I've asked a few of my favorites (including my mom and dad and all three of my brothers) to share what God has done through their lives of open-door legacy. Look for their firsthand stories in the occasional "Extra Helping" sections.

Now in case you were wondering, you don't need to start this journey with an HGTV-designed house (although I wouldn't say no if they offered) or a big, brave declaration. Spic-and-span. Everything in its place. Nor do you need to scour Pinterest for a home-cooked meal or a home-cooked anything. Like me, whenever you open the door, you'll likely be doing it with an overly busy, anxious heart offered to Him, alongside a kitchen counter topped with chips, salsa, and guacamole for good measure. (If you're more of a chocolate girl, I'm good with that too.)

But I'm asking you to toss any preconceived notions aside. Throw out your magazines, cast aside the apprehension, and look at how Jesus modeled this life of welcome. It's going to revolutionize your thought process. Let's reframe our picture of hospitality and discover how God uses simple steps of faithfulness to ignite life change. I'm inviting you to do some hard yet extremely soul-satisfying things with me. I want you to be able to look back in one year, five years—twenty-five years—and glimpse the legacy your footprints have left. I'm already getting excited because I know what awaits. I guarantee it will be worth it.

And I promise, all you have to do is just open the door.

1

What's Hospitality, Really?

A few months ago, I ran into a friend I hadn't seen in years. As we were catching up, she reminisced, "Our son still talks about the tornado party at your house. Remember that? He said it was the best party he'd ever been to."

Remember it? I still shudder thinking about it.

Even in hearing her bring it up, the anxiety of that night flushed all over me again. I could feel the hairs on my back start to cringe (and I'm pretty sure girls aren't supposed to have hair there). That day was one that descended into CHAOS, and by that I mean I felt like defaulting to **C**an't **H**ave **A**nybody **O**ver **S**yndrome. Chaos, I tell you. More than once it brought to mind the saying, "Hospitality is making your guests feel at home, even if you wish they were."

But since we're going to be sharing the good, bad, and ugly of life together in these pages, I'll start with this memory that still makes me shiver, even if now I can chuckle in remembrance.

We live on a large plot of land in the country. Think of the old classic *Green Acres*, starring the city girl who moved with her husband to a wannabe homestead, and that's me . . . minus my dearly departed farm animals, but that's another story. So we're a frequent destination place for our city-suburban friends, especially if they have kids, looking for some wholesome, healthy fun. We've got plenty of that! But what we don't have is a big bonus room or basement with lots of indoor space where the little ones can run wild, so we enjoy having our larger gatherings outside. And that was my plan on the day that became our altogether *un*planned tornado party.

The spectacular North Carolina weather sported mostly blue skies and perfect summer temps. More than seventy-five people had signed up to attend our Sunday school picnic, so I frantically raced against the clock to have everything ready—getting extra chairs and blankets set up outside, dumping soda and ice in the cooler, tending to last-minute details. As the first families pulled in, kids ran for our trampoline while the grown-ups greeted one another with hugs and handshakes, popping the tabs on their favorite cold drinks. This was going to be a blast. I did notice a few dark clouds rolling in, but I'd been checking the weather for days—like I always do—so I wasn't too concerned.

After about fifty people had arrived, I got an SOS text: "Jen, we were halfway to your house and had to turn around. The wind is swirling like crazy and it's pouring. Hail is heading your way too. Did you hear there's a tornado warning for our area?"

Immediately I did the "warning versus watch" check in my mind. I always forget which is which. One of them means a tornado has actually touched down. Which is it? Remembering the difference, I looked at the text again. Yes, she said "warning." We were in serious trouble.

As the thunderclouds raced in, as the winds picked up, as the rain began pelting down, my stomach dropped. We had no choice but to bring everyone inside. What in the world was I going to do with all these kids in the house? Yet no sooner did the challenge present itself than it doubled in intensity. Within a few minutes, just as the skies turned totally black, the power went out. Are you kidding me?

The darkness, though, I could actually deal with. Since candles are my favorite finds at yard sales, I'd accumulated quite a collection, and I rushed to hand them out, lighting up the family room and kitchen. *Hospitality Tip 101:* Candlelight makes everything better, every time. Our home is known for the overkill on candles. It's like white, twinkling lights at Christmastime. Always cozy. But country living also means we have our own well. Our water depends on electricity, which means when we lose power, we lose water, including the water necessary to flush our toilets. So for the next three hours—THREE HOURS!—we basically hosted our fifty-or-so guests with nothing but the use of an indoor porta-potty.

Not knowing what else to do with everyone, I led them in group games, anything I could think of. Parents and kids alike did crazy sing-alongs with the motions they'd learned at church. I'm pretty sure we even sang "The Twelve Days of Christmas"—right there in the middle of July—because when stressed and under pressure, you do what comes to mind. Let's be honest, that song is annoyingly long, and creating time-stretching activities for these kids was my only goal.

I could go on and on with the crazy details. No air-conditioning, no electricity, no flushing toilets. And yet for at least one of the kids who was there, when he thought back on it, he considered it the "best" party ever—because in the midst of total bedlam, we leaned into a level of creativity that never would have surfaced during an outdoor gathering.

The "tornado party" really did turn out to be a memorable event. In fact, my friend's comment was far from the first time I'd heard people speak fondly of it. On that day when I opened our door to the most imperfect hospitality ever served, God opened a door that shifted a lot of our hearts. Many friends throughout the years have pinpointed that day as a significant marker that began shaping their view of true hospitality. Who would have thought? Chaos came in, and grace flowed out. In all its unexpected simplicity.

Hospitality. What is it, really? When we overstress, overplan, and overthink inviting others into our lives and homes, hospitality becomes overwhelming to our souls. We become slaves to the expectations of others. We freeze at the mere thought of extending an invitation. Craving both perfection and polished perception, we fall victim to a cruel taskmaster. So how do we find the balance here? How do we open our door to the unknown without opening ourselves to dread and discouragement?

It comes down to knowing the difference between entertaining and hospitality.

In her flagship book *Entertaining*, Martha Stewart says, "Entertaining, like cooking, is a little selfish, because it really involves pleasing yourself with a guest list that will coalesce into your ideal of harmony, with a menu orchestrated to your home and taste, with decorations subject to your own eye. Given these considerations, it has to be pleasureful."[1]

This one paragraph hints at the telltale difference. It all rests on this dichotomy.

The entertaining host seeks to elevate herself. And as Martha mentions, it's a bit selfish. When the guest arrives, the entertainer announces, "Here I am. Come into my beautiful abode and have the honor of partaking of all the wonderful things I've spent hours getting done for you. Look at this lavish buffet, the intricate décor, and the wonderful party favors. How fortunate for you to be here and be part of this." While I embellish on what a hostess might actually say, we've all encountered this attitude once or twice, haven't we? Maybe we've even allowed a similar tone to slip ever so subtly into our own hosting. But when you leave the entertaining host's house, how do you feel? Remember that, and do the opposite.

Hospitality is different. Biblical hospitality offers our best to Him first, understanding that our best to others will then fall into place. It transforms our selfish motives and elevates our guest. When the hospitable hostess swings wide the door, all her attention focuses outward: "You're here! I've been waiting for you. No one is more important today than you, and I'm thrilled you've come." The posture we assume in hospitality is one that bends low, generously offering our heart to another despite whatever interruption to our own plans or comfort. Extending hospitality is about freely giving of ourselves while granting others the freedom to be themselves. Shifting our focus from us to them removes all unnecessary expectations. No need to worry about what to say or how to act. Just come as you are.

Hospitality, unlike entertaining, treats everyone as a guest of honor rather than grasping at honor for yourself. Opening your door has nothing to do with the actual setting, the guest list, or the food. The atmosphere can be exactly the same yet have very different results based on the heart attitude of the one who welcomes.

Status-seeking versus servanthood.

"Here I am" versus "here you are."

Self-serving to serving others.

Over and over I'm reminded that we have no grand blueprint for hospitality aside from loving others. As the master architect, God drew up hospitality so that it gravitates around this core component—yes, He even determines when we have electricity and when we don't. He is not shy about interrupting our best-laid plans. He will ask us to give up the ordered control we consider so crucial before we'll open the door. But the reason we open the door anyway is because we're driven by the main principles of hospitality: loving Him, loving His will, and following His will into loving others.

The deep-seated worrying, the excuses, and the overthinking of a simple invitation should be warning signs, telling us we're confusing social entertaining with hospitality. When we use our lives exactly as they are, desiring only to create a sacred space for our guests, mixing it with the countercultural truth of loving Jesus and loving others, we turn *entertaining* upside down, and it becomes radical *hospitality*.

As I've studied the ways hospitality is woven throughout the tapestry of Scripture, I've been convicted anew. Beginning in the Old Testament, God tells us to welcome and love the stranger. Within the context of that ancient culture, He instructed His people to give of their time, energy, and whatever meager possessions were on hand, demonstrating hospitality to traveling strangers by feeding and housing them after an exhausting journey. In the New Testament, hospitality is said to be a distinctive mark of the Christian church. Early believers took seriously the command to use their homes as a place for extending grace to others.

Among the most direct, concise biblical statements on this subject is what Paul says in Romans 12:13, "Pursue hospitality." It's not a question. In fact, *pursue* is a strong verb that implies constant or continuous action, a proactive decision. This verse doesn't suggest that some people have the gift of hospitality while others lack it. No, we're all meant to be in the habit of pursuing hospitality. It's a command to love others well in a tangible way. But here's where the blessing comes in. The difference. For as we obey what God commands here—as we begin to experience the fullness, richness, and joy that comes from practicing life-giving hospitality—we see this biblical instruction transforming from an active command to a deep, profound, yet simple calling, one we pursue first out of love, only to find it too contagious for us to stop.

Sweet friend, I know hospitality takes a bold kind of courage, but you can do this. Pursue it with the knowledge that Christ is enough. Whenever you feel, "I can't do this," hear Him remind you, "You're right. You can't. But I can." Hospitality is where He can teach you bold new lessons about trust, humility, faith, and love.

When I replay this truth about God's sufficiency in my heart, confident that He can transform lives in spite of me, all those over-the-top expectations go away. Because, again, it's not about me. I have nothing to prove. He delights to work with my imperfections. If people are blessed and impacted, it's only because He's gracious to take a broken, weary, and unimpressive woman and use her desire for serving Him to point others to Jesus, in spite of herself.

Let this truth sink deep. Receive it as absolute freedom. Stop striving for the unattainable, stop worrying about what others think of your performance, and focus solely on our One-person audience, knowing this focus will always lead you to loving others. If He can work through an indoor porta-potty party, just imagine the other miracles He will perform when you show up and surrender your idea of perfection. Trust me, our version is so overrated anyhow.

So this is it—my simple invitation to awaken your soul to the transforming power of what open-door living can do when you step forward and say, "I'm willing and available."

This book for you may be an invitation to an entirely new way of thinking about hospitality. Or it may be a refresher on what matters most, marked by a new and abiding passion that what you're doing is kingdom work, that you're launching a godly legacy. Either way, you and I will be doing some heart business over these next few chapters. So let's link arms and stop peeking through the window. You hold the key that unlocks the door to so many meaningful possibilities, and I can't wait to discover them with you.

Baby steps, sweet sister. The road of welcome awaits.

And it's sure to take you and your guests to some of the "best" moments and memories you've ever had.

Coming to the end of this chapter (and every chapter), enjoy a couple of extra features that I hope will help you process and implement what God is encouraging you to do as you read. "Dear Jen" is a brief Q&A initiated by some of my blog readers. "Elevate the Ordinary" includes specific tips and ideas that can take you from "not me" to "Yes, I can do that too!"

Dear Jen

While the thought of hosting a large group paralyzes me, I love the idea of inviting a few friends for an outdoor picnic, yet I don't want to worry about cooking. What's your favorite suggestion?

Newbie

Dear Newbie,

As you take your first step, set yourself up for success and don't bother attempting a full dinner. Instead, enjoy a good old-fashioned ice cream social. Gather lawn games, ask people to bring their favorite topping or ice cream flavor, and assemble an evening topped with sweetness. Or go for the gold by building the "world's longest" banana split. Purchase a plastic rain gutter and run it on top of your tables. Using the gutter as the big bowl, each guest creates their favorite ice cream sundae side by side. Kids love this, and they'll talk about it for years (especially if you're extra generous with the whipped cream and cherries).

Jen

Elevate the Ordinary

❀ Have you been meaning to text or call a certain friend for weeks, but you've been putting it off? Stop now, grab your phone, and let her know you're thinking of her.

❀ Create a friendly and inviting front-door area. Clear all miscellaneous clutter. If you have space, consider painting a cute wooden chair or bench and setting a basket of flowers on top. I found mine for five dollars at a yard sale. Or maybe be bold and give the door a fresh, new paint color. You won't believe the difference it makes.

❀ My favorite way to greet guests is by personalizing a message to them on this huge chalkboard I made. And it's so easy to do. At a thrift store, purchase the largest framed picture you can find, spray paint the frame white, then paint over the picture with chalkboard paint. Voila! Now you can greet each guest with a warm, personalized welcome.

Open-Door Invitations

I know this is unusual, maybe reckless or even unsafe in this sin-filled world. But the truth is that I've lived many decades with an actual open front door in my home . . . yes, even at night!

Along the way, I've had a big husband, three strong sons, and plenty of live-in guests as protectors—which is helpful, since having a locked door hasn't been on the top of my must-do list.

Just as I've had a physical open door in my life, I've tried to keep my spiritual door open as well, and this has given me a lifetime of surprise guests. Usually, these guests were spiritually troubled in some way, and God repeatedly brought them into my life through that open door! After multiple occurrences, it's become apparent to me that these random visitors weren't accidental at all. Actually, I believe these experiences are how God has used my life's desire to serve Him more fully with each remaining day.

One of the first visitors we welcomed through our front door was a young, pregnant girl who lived two and a half hours away from us. She arrived with her embarrassed parents one Sunday afternoon, needing a home during the showing stage of her pregnancy. Overwhelming love flooded our hearts, and she became like a daughter to us to shepherd through some heart-wrenching months leading up to the birth of her precious baby girl. Thirty-plus years later, our bond with this special "daughter" remains stronger than ever.

Another opportunity to offer hospitality occurred immediately after I had returned home from my first of eight mission trips to China as an ESL teacher (English as a Second Language). The Chinese people had found a lasting place in my heart, so when I returned home, I reached out to local universities to find a Chinese woman who was interested in being a language friendship partner with an American woman. Soon after, I was introduced to a Chinese student and arranged to meet with her for coffee. We clicked immediately as my spiritual front door opened, and both of us knew this was the beginning of something special. She was divorced with a young son in a strange country, and she needed help with a custody battle, a difficult process in the male-dominated Chinese culture. After retaining a Christian lawyer, we methodically walked through a difficult court case with her. A few years later, she remarried and in time gave birth to a precious baby girl. Needing to return to her work as an accountant, she gave me the joy and privilege of caring for her baby for seven months until the family was transferred to another city. A lifetime connection again!

A next example occurred when one of our married sons was spending a lot of time working out in the gym. He met another young married man (with a son) who'd been removed from his home by his wife because of his drug addiction. Our son offered our home to him as a halfway location during his rehab period. Because of all our previous live-ins, our son felt comfortable in issuing this invite. So we met the young man for lunch. And after hearing his account, in which he admitted his own guilt in the situation, we decided to honor our son's invite and give him a chance. He was a schoolteacher, and before leaving our home every morning, he would check in with us and announce that he was "clean" (our rule). Unfortunately, there were some setbacks along the way, but we carried on in anticipation of his victory. He was with us for about a year when he was finally set free from his addiction. He and his wife repeated their marriage vows, and they were once again reunited as a family.

The list of other visitors is too long to mention here. But our door is still open! Our home actually feels empty whenever we are without God's surprise guests. Who might be next? We don't know, but He does!

2

Trickle Down

My husband ran to stop the elevator door before it could close on us. As he held it open, I struggled to maneuver our double stroller through the opening. Bumping against one side, then the other, I finally brought it to a resting point, while the passengers who were already inside bunched themselves closer together to make way. "So sorry," I apologized, my eyes glancing down at our two boys, giggling from their mini bumper car ride.

A Saturday night on the town, even if only to window shop at the local mall, was worth the chaotic adventure. As a momma of littles—two under two—my outings had been mostly confined to the grocery store, where the highlights of my afternoon were free balloons and cookie samples. Earlier that morning, I'd been so bleary-eyed from being up late the night before, I *may* have smeared leftover baby food on our breakfast toast. I *may* have drunk warm milk with graham cracker crumbs floating in it. And I *may* have actually considered it my special treat for the day. The nights weren't much better. I would lie awake during the 2:00 a.m. feeding and ponder my pre-baby days, back when I used to question deep metaphysical aspects about the universe. Now in post-baby days, I considered my twentieth reading of *Goodnight Moon* as a form of astronomy study and felt pretty good about myself. It all counts, right? I never was much of a math and science girl.

But on this night, my husband and I were out on a mall adventure, only three weeks after saying good-bye to family, our jobs, our church home, a lifetime of shared memories, and many deeply rooted relationships, moving across the country from Wisconsin to North Carolina. I'd experienced a lot of life with my friends back home. They'd transitioned with me from single, to married, to new mom. They'd walked with me through my highs and lows—loved me through confrontation, leaned into life when it was fun and easy, yet hadn't run the other way when times grew tough. We'd cried together through hurt and sickness and laughed our way through late-night Oreo and French fry binges (my favorite food). I knew we'd been called to make this move to North Carolina, but—exhausted, homesick, and isolated—I still struggled with starting all over.

And now I stood here wedged against a family of total strangers in an elevator car, my emotions running as high as my awkward discomfort for crowding into their space.

My husband broke the ice by commenting on the dad's Pittsburgh Steelers shirt. There's something about men and their hometown football allegiances that creates instant community. In the few seconds between our getting on board and the elevator doors opening three floors later, these guys had bonded over exchanged Packers and Steelers stories. It's so simple for them.

But by next morning, I'd learned an entirely new lesson in simple. I learned how simple it is for God to orchestrate even our most spontaneous moments. And how a simple invitation can change everything.

As we were picking up our toddler from his new Sunday school classroom, guess who caught my eye across the hall? I couldn't believe it—our mall elevator acquaintances from the night before! What were the chances?

But the fun didn't stop there—because no sooner had we made the connection and laughed at our uncanny reunion, they said something that breathed life into a weary-souled momma who needed a reminder that God cared about all my little, seemingly superficial details. "I know it's last minute and we just met, but would your family like to come over for lunch today?" Without any preplanning or overthinking, without taking time to worry if their home was clean or if they had a meal ready to go, our elevator friends extended an invitation to relative strangers.

Today? Right now? I was stunned, surprised, grateful, and overwhelmed by this simple act of kindness—a symbolic lifeline extended when I needed it most.

Their home was cozy and humble. They lived on the husband's public school teacher's salary, so there were no frills, no extras. Yet we gathered lunch meat for sandwiches and made boxed pasta to stretch the meal. It was nothing but wonderful. That afternoon, their hearts rolled out the red carpet for our exhausted crew, and their life-giving hospitality welcomed us into community.

Two decades have passed since that Sunday afternoon meal—a simple exchange that became a remembrance marker of sorts, a tangible demonstration of God's love to me. At a time when I felt so alone, He knew I craved a reminder of His constant compassion, and through our new friends' obedience to extend hospitality, God clearly revealed His character to this momma barely hanging on.

That's the heart of hospitality: to point others to Him, to love on one another while affirming His goodness.

As women, our souls ache for an invitation to be included and welcomed. We possess a hidden longing for rooted relationships that journey through life with us. We need someone to notice, acknowledge, and see us right where we are, with no hidden agenda. God has designed us to come together in community, whether large or small.

And while we were made to belong to one another, this core extension of ourselves has been lost in modern society. Somehow we've dressed up this simple desire to gather, and we've laced it with imposing expectations and the pressure of performance. We've packed the calendar so full of busyness that it's created unnecessary bondage, making the concept of margin merely a myth. Why have we made community so difficult? And how do we—how do I—help bring back what's been lost?

When guests walk through the door to my house, the first thing they see is a sign hanging on the wall. Personalized with our family name, the Schmidts, it goes on to say:

Delighted you are here.
Welcome to a place where we
celebrate both the beauty and bedlam.

It's a play off my blog name, *Balancing Beauty and Bedlam*, where for nearly ten years I've encouraged women to join me in the daily dance of seeking out magical moments hidden among the seemingly mundane, those simple treasures found within the daily chaos.

When I first started this blog, I was knee-deep in the throes of mothering and often felt like I was a step behind everyone else. I was feeling the challenge and pressure of trying to embrace it all. So instead of highlighting a quest for perfection resulting in a hamster wheel of failure, the blog was my reminder to practice the discipline of celebrating the little things in life, which are often the big moments where true joy awaits.

Over nearly a decade, this sign that speaks of "beauty" amid the "bedlam" welcomed more than a thousand guests through our side door—the door that opens into our laundry room. Yes, you read that correctly. When guests came into our home, they walked directly through our laundry room. That was never my intention. Our first year's home goal included paying cash to build a porch, big enough for outdoor parties yet cozy enough for afternoon tea. That was the plan, but sometimes our best laid plans aren't His, you know? For years we didn't have the funds to invest back in our house or even finish our front walkway, so the side entrance access became easy and familiar.

Early on, I did my best to pretty her up with a quaint antique chandelier I found at the thrift store, but it was still a tiny laundry room complete with a washer, dryer, and rows of shelving stacked with muddy shoes. I made excuses and apologized for the mess, knowing it didn't measure up with many of the homes I'd visited. But as the lure of this comparison trap intertwined with my desire to prove something, I acknowledged my pride as sin and declared that I would not let it steal from me the sweet blessing of community I craved or my responsibility and privilege as a Christ follower to multiply that joy with as many people as possible. I refused to allow my delight in welcoming others disintegrate because of the crazy lies swirling in my head. Trust me, I realize this is so much easier said than done. I'm constantly asking the Lord to shift my motives back to Him, while fighting against my own desire to first impress others rather than solely bless them. It doesn't happen overnight.

When we least expect it, comparison sneaks up like a thief and attempts to rob us of all joy, especially when it pertains to things as personal as our home. And you know what—no one has time for that.

It's exhausting enough making sure the toilet seat is down and the bathroom is clean, without the arrows of comparison taking target practice on our "Martha wannabe" skills. Perfection is the enemy of done. Wait, forget that, sometimes perfection is the enemy of even starting.

So right then, I determined to replace lies with the truth. I chose to remind myself of our home's desired purpose, which has nothing to do with appearances. Then I set it to words:

> May our home be a safe, refreshing haven where everyone is loved, valued, and welcome; a soft place to land where real life happens. When guests arrive, may they sense a joyful "Welcome Home" spirit that points them to Christ, and may it permeate in such a way that every single person feels as if they can truly make themselves at home.

But it's the next sentence—the closing sentence—that chokes me up as I read it again now. Because although I wrote it more than a decade ago, here I am today, watching these words come full circle, as I now have the privilege of ushering them to you.

> Our home is a place where everyone is welcome, yet may I never wait until I'm ready to swing those doors wide open, because if I wait, it will never happen.

"Swing those doors wide open." Even then I was preaching "just open the door" to my own heart, while identifying with the difficult truth that if left to my own timing, I will never be ready. I can always find an excuse, a reason, a justifiable explanation for why we'll get together "next time." How about you?

Honestly, opening the door may mean prying it open. Sometimes obedience requires a chisel to set things in motion. But all good things take a little work, right? I can't begin to express how much a small inconvenience now impacts the long-term vision of spreading community in, out, and all around. It's always well worth the effort.

Here I am in my later forties now (gasp), able to personally testify to the blessed effects of hospitality on three distinct generations and life stages—my parents; my husband and myself, as well as my three siblings; and now my own children and our slew of nieces and nephews.

This story would be so different had I written it years ago. I've seen hospitality practiced by people of varying financial means and social backgrounds (our own family has experienced a range of financial brackets ourselves), as well as people of differing gifts and personalities. I've practiced hospitality myself in the finest American homes and the tiniest Bangkok apartments. I've gathered at tables across four continents, from Third-World thatched huts in Peru to high-rise "castles" in Southeast Asia. I've cooked outdoor meals over hot coals near the Amazon and enjoyed industrial-sized ovens in Europe. I've served dinner on boxes, as well as on fine china. I've been both welcomed and rebuffed, both respected and betrayed. All of it.

But through every exchange, I can still declare, "It's all worth it." It truly is. While I've gathered a wealth of tried-and-true takes on what works and what doesn't, there's no one right way to do it, and doing it today looks a little bit different than it did yesterday. Every one of our circumstances is unique, but one thing remains true across the board: living a life committed to kingdom-purpose intentionality will mark your life in untold ways.

Three Sundays had passed since we'd enjoyed that impromptu lunch with our new "elevator" friends. I'd found a new rhythm, along with a new desire to include others as I had been included. So after church, when we stopped in the gym to let the boys run and crawl out their energy (boy moms unite! open gym for everyone!), a young couple entered right behind us with their own little boy. This was their first week visiting, they said. And it was my chance now to flip the script from three weeks ago.

We chatted for a while. The guys talked football; we girls bonded over our lack of sleep. Then—just like it happened before—without any preplanning or overthinking, without taking time to worry if our home was clean or if I had a meal ready to go, I extended an invitation to relative strangers. "I know it's last minute and we just met," I said, "but would your family like to come over for lunch today?" And with the same sense of gratitude I'd felt when we'd been on the receiving end of that question ourselves, this family took us up on the offer as well.

It didn't end there. It rarely does. This invitation led to a friendship, which led to doing life together in a couple's small group where we wrestled with questions such as, How will I survive raising these blessings without an instruction guide? Not only did we survive, but we did it through years made so much richer because of the people with whom God allowed us to link arms.

Not long ago I was telling my daughter the full-circle story of how we'd first met these dear friends in the church gym some twenty years ago. I'd recently run into the wife and mom of the family while at a concert. I heard my name called. Then she said to her friend, "Oh, I want you to meet someone." As part of introducing me, she said, "Jen and Gregg were the first people we met here. They invited us over on the spot and welcomed us immediately. We've never forgotten that. It made such an impact."

My daughter couldn't believe I'd never shared with her the story of that initial invitation because she vividly remembers those Friday evening small groups we hosted that included these friends. Nor could I believe that in recalling it, I found myself choked up, overwhelmed by a wave of unexpected emotion. I guess it caught me at a moment when, in the midst of life's chaos and complexity, I had sort of lost touch with how much a simple extension of Christ's love toward others can affect them. Rarely do we see the outcome, but in this case I did.

I wish I could say the tears trickling down my face that day were shed from sweet sentiments, although maybe that was some of it. But more than anything, they were tears born out of a gut-wrenching conviction for times when I'd failed to recognize the trickle-down effect of hospitality in God's economy. How many other simple invitations had I left unextended? How often had I closed the door on life-giving exchanges without even realizing it?

Something about that moment, that memory, sparked a mini spiritual revival in me. I begged the Lord to awaken my heart once again, to sensitize my spirit to the needs of those around me, to guide me in the rediscovery of hidden gems of hospitality where I'd become complacent. And He has. I'm tuned in. I'm listening. I'm alert.

After decades of following Him, I've discovered again that open-door living has such a ripple effect, such an impact on how we all experience the sense of community He desires for us. One invitation can lead down so many roads . . . ones that are paved with something so much greater than good intentions.

Dear Jen

We live in a really small apartment, and I struggle with hosting because there's not a lot of room for people. Do you have suggestions for small-living hospitality?

Tiny Living

Dear Tiny Living,

I remember those days well. I hosted many people in our tiny apartment, and it's worth getting creative with your space limitations. First, push furniture against the walls to make more room. Gather any breakables as well as miscellaneous clutter and put in a plastic bin. (I admit, sometimes I needed two.) Move them to the bedroom for the evening. I even put our extra coffee table there since it wasn't needed. Use your patio or grassy area for additional space, and focus on keeping things simple. My motto is K.I.S.S.—Keep It Sweet and Simple. If you invite a larger group to your apartment, consider starting inside for drinks and appetizers, and then take your meal outdoors to the apartment's common area, or use the clubhouse. If your complex has a pool or other amenities, use those too, and invite guests for a poolside gathering.

Before I had children, I always kept a small bin of toys for guests with kids. This kept them occupied because everyone loves to play with something new. Once we had children, I continued with the same concept and used our "guest-only bin" for special occasions. Our kids enjoyed having company because they looked forward to playing with new friends and new-to-them toys. (Just don't tell where you hide them.)

Jen

Elevate the Ordinary

❀ Can you think of one friend or family you could invite for lunch this weekend? It doesn't have to be at your home—maybe at a local restaurant—but extend the invitation. Just start.

❀ Or maybe you're ready to go all in for a spontaneous, Sunday challenge. Put on a big pot of Dump & Run Taco Soup[2] or buy a pan of frozen lasagna and invite someone on the spot. You may get a few no's before a yes, so don't get discouraged. Keep welcoming.

❀ Are you struggling with the appearance of your worn-out furniture but don't have the budget to purchase all-new pieces? Never underestimate the power of mixed textures on sofas and chairs. I draped a beautiful blanket over the edge of our worn club chair, which disguised the ripped corner seamlessly. Then by layering a simple white chenille bedspread over our dated brown sofa and adding a pop of color with new throw pillows, I turned an outdated corner into a cute, cozy gathering spot.

3

The Do-Over

The reminder to "just start" is a powerful one. It frees us to get our feet wet in learning to live a life of welcome. But you know what I appreciate even more than "just start"?

The do-over.

Yes, I am a big fan. The idea of getting a clean slate. A fresh start. After all the ways I can mess things up. Bring it on.

And on one particular Wednesday night, my do-over couldn't come soon enough.

With girlfriends set to arrive in an hour, I scurried around trying to set the dining room table. But from my peripheral vision, I witnessed pockets of the family room that were completely uninhabitable.

"Everyone get down here now," I called upstairs to whoever could hear me. When my appeal didn't elicit a response, I threw my inside voice aside and screeched a little louder—where *everyone* could hear. "I mean it! I gave you plenty of time to clean up this mess, and I am ticked! Those ladies are coming shortly, so stuff everything you can in the closets! When they're full, run anything else upstairs!" (Yes, this is why I have a "no adult guests upstairs" rule. Heaven forbid it looks like five kids live here.)

I could feel my internal pressure cooker about to blow. I'd created a frenzied schedule with no margin carved into my day and then invited guests into my already crowded soul space. With my patience nearly nonexistent, I needed to get this stuff done immediately. Why do I always do this to myself? There wasn't anything I could change now. The do-betters would need to wait.

With my kids now picking up and momma doing ten things at once, I tasked our twelve-year-old son to finish making the taco dip. This wasn't anything out of the ordinary. It's pretty much a dinner staple at our house, so he could make it by heart. All I needed was for him to chop the green pepper, add it into the sour cream mixture, and spread the dip on the cute platter I'd already laid out. Easy-peasy. I only had one simple request: "Make sure you only chop the green pepper—this one right here." I held it up and placed it by the knife. "That other one, the habanero, is so hot, it'll burn someone's mouth."

Okay? Okay.

But isn't this a flashback of something similar we've heard before? "Taylor, you can ~~eat~~ chop any fruit in the garden, just not this one. Or else . . ." No? Just me? Okay then, moving on.

With this simple five-minute chore assigned, I felt free to finish my speed cleaning, knowing my main appetizer was in good hands. As soon as I'd set out the desserts and appetizers and completed a last-minute sink swipe and toilet flush, I was ready to welcome. Here they came.

And everything was going along great—people laughing and catching up, everyone piling their plates with goodies. Then I heard it. The first dreaded gasp. "Can I have some water?" Another chimed in, "Me too." Then another. And another.

No.

He didn't.

He wouldn't.

Oh my word, he did!

Suddenly I knew what had happened. Laden with a mixture of green *AND* habanero peppers, the taco dip was exploding in my company's collective mouths. Grabbing a pitcher of cold water and apologizing profusely, I excused myself and stormed into our son's room, where four of our children were watching TV.

"Are you kidding me? How in the world could you even *think* about doing that? Do you have any idea what you did?" Seething, the screaming was soft, under my breath, not wanting our guests to hear me through the air vents. But from the words I *did* manage to get out, I pretty much accused him of lacing the taco dip with arsenic. It wasn't one of my prouder mothering moments—my humanity on full display for all my favorite humans, our children. I barged out of the room, leaving them in stunned silence.

Returning to my guests, I explained our son's inappropriate practical joke. They graciously understood ("boys," they nodded), chuckled even. But the unconfessed carnage my words had leveled against him from moments earlier wouldn't leave me.

I needed to find him. An immediate do-over was in order. I knew I couldn't wipe it all clean. But I'd try my best.

As I opened his door, he immediately cried out, "Mom, I'm so sorry. I shouldn't have done that. I knew it was wrong." I wrapped him in my arms and begged his forgiveness too, as we simultaneously expressed both our love and regret. I gathered all the kids and apologized for my attitude.

If they're going to embrace open-door living, I never want them to associate welcoming others into our heart and home with a crazed mother who loses it for the sake of "pursuing hospitality." I do want them observing a mom who loves others well, sometimes messes up her priorities in the process, yet wants to keep giving it another try.

Whenever do-overs present themselves, I run for the opportunity. Life is too short not to embrace them. There's nothing like the new-found gratitude of grace that comes from second chances, mixed with the anticipation of new beginnings.

But the thing about do-overs is that there's no guarantee you'll get them.

I was struck by this reality again one afternoon on our back patio, as the sun set on a conversation I was having with a dear friend. I looked into her face as she paged through her journal, sharing glimpses of her private thoughts with me—prayers she'd cried, Scriptures she'd penned, truths the Lord had revealed to her. Barely a month earlier, her eldest son—the nineteen-year-old who'd made her a mom—had gone to be with the Lord. And here she was now, having endured such a horrific tragedy, grasping to understand, seeking to heal, submitting with complete, surrendered dependence on our heavenly Father.

Not a day goes by that I don't think of my friend and her family and how temporary our days on earth truly are. She and I both had three stair-step boys followed by a girl (for us, followed by another girl), and the nightmare call she received—the one every parent dreads—could just as easily have been placed to me. Her experience is such a sobering reminder. We blink, time ticks, and it doesn't come back again. And yet when the available opening of a do-over moment does occur, it's as though God is giving us an opportunity to turn back the clock, providing us a humble, grace-filled, and powerful way to redeem the time.

God has a way of using our all-too-human failings as tools that *refine* us—the would've, could've, should've, everyday moments where we failed to remember that each person and interaction is precious. What we do with our next choices, with our do-overs, is what will *define* us. Do-overs mean we get to decide how to mark these finite moments going forward.

The messy kitchen, the dented car, the overlooked promotion, the hot pepper in the dip. By implementing the power of the do-over, earlier annoyances turn into holy moments. Grumbling becomes gratitude. Formerly big things slip harmlessly away into obscurity.

So I'm urging you now, same as the Lord urged me through the eye-opener of that painful loss in my friend's family, to take a do-over. No regrets. Leave the past behind and focus on being intentional with your next steps. Lean into a perspective shift that will define your future choices, especially when it comes to open-door living. For me, it's meant the simplicity of a one-word shift in my vocabulary. It's such a slight change really, yet it turns all this making of meals and tending of wounds, all this continuing to serve when I'm tired and worn out and don't really want to do it anymore—it turns it all into a privilege.

And here's the one-word difference. Swap out every "have to" for a "get to."

"I don't have to; I get to."

Let this simple shift in perspective become your war cry. Whether married, single, mothers or not, take a one-word gratitude challenge that will impact how you do life with those around you. When discontentment begins to settle in your heart, turn a "have to" attitude into a "get to" attitude, and it will elevate your ability to press in and learn to love what needs to be done, regardless of how you feel. Start cultivating a garden of "get to" moments:

"I don't *have* to _____; I *get* to."

- "I don't *have* to tackle the laundry load; I *get* to." Thankful we have a washer that does the extra hard work.
- "I don't *have* to go to work; I *get* to." Thankful to be employed and able to earn a paycheck.
- "I don't *have* to listen and engage with my difficult neighbor; I *get* to." She has a story to be told. And to really listen to what she's saying means to love her.
- "I don't *have* to host these missionaries; I *get* to." What a privilege to support people who are sacrificially living out the Great Commission.

Leading with gratitude opens up the floodgates to all kinds of hospitality, making you content with the small things you have to offer while increasing your desire to share them with others. Whatever you've done before and however you've chosen to do it, changing your "have to" to "get to" is like getting a whole new do-over.

For me personally, it's changed how I open the door to those in my own family. I've started saying yes, for example, to a lot more seemingly simple (even silly) things, marking them as moments that matter to the people who share my home. I've given myself permission to loosen up, to be fun and crazy for the sole reason that I'm over-the-top loved by my Savior. I'm dancing in the kitchen like no one's watching. (Although when you have teens, they secretly post the embarrassing videos online, so be careful.) I'm squirting whipped cream straight into our mouths— my kids' mouths, their friends' mouths, as well as my own mouth—and every once in a while, right on their noses. I'm taking walks in the woods with our girls and leaving the phone behind. I'm snuggling on their beds for late-night conversation. And recently this mom who hates road trips embraced spontaneity and drove four hours for a fun mother/daughter overnight.

But one of the best things? Nearly every time they ask to have their friends over, I say yes—because these days are flying by, and I want them to want to be here . . . here at home, our greatest mission field, where we don't even have to go anywhere to watch the Lord at work. That's because only two things remain in the end: God's Word and our relationships. And I want to be right in the stream of it all. Saying "I get to" instead of "I have to" keeps me investing in other people, the kind of investment that really matters and reaps the greatest rewards long after I'm gone.

On the morning of the funeral, the day my friend would be burying her son, my own son stumbled down the stairs for breakfast. I had a nice, hot plate of eggs waiting for him. But he didn't want eggs. He wanted pancakes. What do I look like, a short-order cook?

But with a broken heart for a grieving mother, I recognized the sunrise of a do-over day. No, I didn't "have to" change gears and prepare my son a stack of homemade pancakes with berry love. I "get to" do it—a privilege my precious friend would've given anything to do that morning. What a gift from God that I could take a do-over, right that moment, on this back-breaking, soul-draining journey of motherhood—this open-door calling on my life that I consider such a privilege. May I never see it any other way.

The greatest of all do-overs is one we get to experience every day as followers of Jesus, natural-born rebels rescued from the guilt and shame of our sin by the forgiving mercy and grace of God. He has given us, because of His abundant, faithful love for us, the ultimate do-over.

And so if anything sums up our basis for wanting to do things over, such as resolving to embrace a more open-door lifestyle, the one word behind this motivation is simple too. It's *love*. Love is our invitation to act.

We throw the word *love* around like it's our favorite stuffed animal. We love coffee. We love chocolate. We love a good book. We love Netflix. But no love compares to the love Jesus spoke about in answer to this question from one of the Pharisees: "'Teacher, which command in the law is the greatest?' He said to him, 'Love the Lord your God with all your heart, with all your soul, and with all your mind. This is the greatest and most important command. The second is like it: Love your neighbor as yourself. All the Law and the Prophets depend on these two commands'" (Matt. 22:36–40).

In other words, everything good that His Spirit produces in our lives comes from a single-minded devotion to these two priorities: to love God and to love others.

Love God. Too often the things I love center around *me*. Sometimes even the way I choose to show my love for God subtly shifts back to me. Ack! Why do I do that? When I slay my self-tendencies and remain laser-focused on Him, I'm deeply aware of my need for a Savior, which is exactly where He wants me—exactly where He wants all of us. What He asks is profoundly simple: Love Him. Yet there's a power struggle, a fierce competition going on for captivating our whole hearts because we're preoccupied with all things self. The culture screams, *Produce! Accomplish! Succeed!* So we jump in and strive, reach, and grab, all in the attempt to do more, be more, and make more. Comparison's stranglehold plays games with our self-image, so we build our identity on others' expectations, rubbing against God's view of us: beloved, cherished, and worthy. Our feelings, though valuable gifts that help us experience life, are notoriously horrible captains. If we allow altered emotions to steer us, it's a crash waiting to happen. Wholeheartedly loving God and believing the truth that He loves us infinitely more than we can ever imagine requires that we anchor our feelings in His Word and keep careful watch over what fills our hearts and minds. He knows if He's captivated our hearts, He'll have control of everything else too. Only with a heart fully alive in Him, one that dances in the freedom He offers and celebrates this abundant life as someone who knows they're truly loved, can His next command even sound possible.

Love others. Let's be super honest for a minute because I'm a shoot-straight, no pretending kind of girl. Loving certain people is brutal. It doesn't come naturally. Often our desire is to give and receive love but only by the pretty, the popular, the lovable. That's cheap love. Easy love. A cleaned-up, less messy version of authentically loving our neighbor that doesn't cost us anything.

Yet we are called (no, commanded) to love the unlovable. Not just love them but love them well. But isn't that what we all are? Unlovable?

And isn't that what Christ has done for us? Loved us well? I like how C. S. Lewis puts it: "The rule for all of us is pretty simple. Do not waste time bothering whether you 'love' your neighbor; act as if you did."[3] We do have a choice of whether or not we'll love others as we love ourselves. And a rekindled commitment to open-door living is one of the primary graces God gives us to shove our selfish, judging, overly critical resistance out of the way and put His love into action.

There's no separating these two instructions: to love God and love others. No divided allegiances here. Jesus didn't even pause, like He could have, before presenting these twin commandments as a united whole. The way we love our neighbor reveals something about the way we love God. And the way we love God reveals something about the way we love our neighbor.

Let's sit on the gravity of this for a minute. The Great Commandment rests on this cornerstone: loving God and loving others.

Not because we "have to" but because we "get to."

Oh friend, I want my love for God and His love for me to spill out to those around me in such a tangible way that they can't help but wonder what makes me different.

Don't you want the same?

In light of this, is there anything you'd like to do over?

Because I know I want to get this right.

Dear Jen

I can find any number of excuses not to invite people into my home, which makes it even harder because my husband is similar. He's definitely a "have to" rather than a "get to" kind of guy. But you've challenged me to step outside my comfort zone, and I really want to try.

Looking back, I see opportunities I missed, and although I know I can't go back and change the past, I can begin now with a do-over. What are your suggestions for someone whose spouse isn't thrilled to open their house to community?

I Want To (but not there yet)

Dear I Want To,

Oh my, I feel as if I may be stepping into a land mine with this one, so please don't hand this to your husband and tell him, "Jen said so."

1. Since situations and family dynamics differ, I direct these questions to you: When you decide to open your home, how much work is he responsible for? Do you give him a "honey do" list a mile long? Does the expectation of hosting come with hours' worth of assigned work alongside heightened tensions to get the house ready? After an exhausting workweek, find ways for him to look forward to enjoying time with friends, not dread it. It's about connection, not perfection, so we must remember: hospitality versus entertaining.

2. If he is still resistant, begin by having your girlfriends over so that he doesn't have to participate or do anything at all to get ready. Let him see that you value community without unnecessary expectations placed on him.

3. Pray for wisdom to know the right time and the right way to talk to him about it.

4. When you finally do talk with him, lead with a humble heart. Show him respect as you unpack some of the things you're learning, and let him know you'd love hosting as a couple/family. Look for a compromise that's fun for both of you.

Jen

Elevate the Ordinary

❀ Create your own "I don't have to _____; I get to" list. Stick it on the fridge as a reminder of your one-word perspective shift.

❀ Is there a do-over in your own life you may need to embrace? It's never too late for an apology and the grace of second chances.

❀ Praise music makes chores more manageable. Turn on some dance music, get your moves on, and spend ten minutes clearing off the kitchen counters and main surfaces. Your day will feel significantly lighter when that simple task is completed. You'll wonder why you didn't do it sooner, and you may decide it's the perfect day to invite a neighbor over for coffee at your clean table.

4

Hospitality on the Go

$\mathcal{M}$y Norman Rockwell image of cozy, home-based hospitality was drop-kicked into the end zone when I first realized that Jesus, the One we model hospitality after, never owned a home. Yep, ponder that for a minute. Jesus, who embodied the ultimate lifestyle of hospitality—the guru, the style guide, the living portrait of all things welcome—did not own a home.

Anything I know about gathering people, I learned from Him. And yet He never stayed in one place. He always traveled where needed and met people where they were, sometimes in the most unlikely places. He walked the road of welcome and offered the gift of invitation wherever, whenever, and with whomever He came in contact. Everywhere He went He initiated hospitality. *Come and see*, He invited as He traveled. *Follow Me*, He instructed the disciples. *Come eat with Me*, as He opened His life with an invitation to draw near. *Walk with Me, sit with Me, and rest*, as He welcomed those weary. *Come drink*, as He poured out life-giving water.[4]

We learn to make room for one more because He first made room for one more. We invite and gather because He did it first. This most amazing host, the One who teaches what it means to invite others into a new way of life, never had a permanent address, yet He is the embodiment of all things home. This should be an "aha" moment for many of us. Jesus always created a safe place of belonging. Even we ourselves, through His invitation, have been chosen and welcomed, yet He was essentially homeless on earth and relied on others' hospitality as well.

So, how do we take our cue from Jesus and take our hospitality on the road?

For me, it all started on the football field.

We're a football family. My dad played it; my husband played it. We grew up with the Packers as the emblem of community, and ever since our boys could toddle, they turned any kind of ball into a football. Toss them a soccer ball, and they played football. Grab some sticks, and end zones formed.

And now their day was finally here. Our seven- and eight-year-old sons ran into the house, stumbling over each other's words as each tried being the first to give me the details. They were signing up to play football, and their contagious, energetic excitement bubbled over. They couldn't have been happier when, after a little discussion about responsibility and sacrifice and elementary-school time management, we handed back the signed checks and football papers (which I believe included some kind of blood oath in the small print). I was happy for them, I really was. But when I looked more carefully at that schedule—three practices a week and games on Saturdays—I saw that life as I knew it was about to change. Hijacked without notice. I thought it was too much, and I set out to let everyone know it.

"What kind of parents put this much time into sports?" I ranted. "This is how families get themselves all out of whack, by turning things like football into an idol. The amount of time this is going to cost us is ridiculous." Talk about someone with a chip on her shoulder. Mine was mountainous.

I stewed with resentment for the first few weeks until one day it was as though the Lord pounded me (it was football after all), saying something like, "Jen, knock it off. You signed up for this and agreed to this schedule, so quit complaining and wasting time. Choose to bring Me glory in the midst of it."

Yes, sometimes the Lord tackles us in the end zone when we need it most.

So I made a conscious choice right then and there to alter my attitude, to lean into the schedule to which we had committed. I released my previous plans for those free football hours and offered them to the Lord. *Remember, Jen, you don't have to; you get to.*

For the next few months, the sidelines became my new home, and the families involved became my people. I packed up my love of hospitality and brought it with me to the football field, while the Lord and I exchanged a few high-fives over the idea that this is where He'd placed me for this season. Different nationalities, different social and economic backgrounds, varying political affiliations—He'd brought them all to this field and put them right in front of me. "Look what you 'get to' do," I could almost hear Him saying, "Go have fun!"

That year was revolutionary. I approached practice time with an elevated vision. I'd sit on the bleachers, on the sidelines, or behind the concession stands, wondering, *Whom can I love on today? Who needs encouragement?* Nothing fancy. No special skills needed. No agenda. I started paying attention. I brought blankets, snacks, and toys for our babies and asked other moms to join me. The blanket became our table and the two-hour practice a lifeline of new community. Even on those days when this momma arrived worn and weary, I had no special expectation except, *I'm here. Come sit if you want.* As I looked to my right and then to my left, women sitting beside me needed the love of Jesus, and I knew how to share it because I needed it myself. And let me tell you, He started showing up in that place, right there over the kids' Goldfish crackers and applesauce.

Later in the season, a few of us started a walking group instead of sitting the whole time. We formed a special bond (plus, I was in the best shape since I'd been married—great benefit) as we walked in circles around the field. With this new vision, I challenged myself with the Rule of Three: each practice, talk to three new people I didn't know. (It might feel awkward at first, but trust me, it really does get easier the more you do it. Start with, "Which child out there is yours?" "How are you managing this crazy schedule?" "Any suggestions for getting dinner on the table? Oh, you're struggling with that as well? Me too.") By the end of the season, I'd interacted with nearly everyone on those sidelines.

Full disclosure, I'm no martyr. There were days when I sat in my chair, head down, flipping through magazines and communicating through my body language, "Don't even think about talking to me." We all have those days, right? But for the most part, I took Jesus' example seriously and learned to walk the road of welcome throughout these everyday, ballpark interactions in my life.

It's a pretty radical concept. Hospitality as an on-the-go lifestyle. Hospitality: will travel. But since when has anything Jesus modeled turned out to be anything less than radical?

Please don't underestimate this. Living on mission is a powerful force. He has called, equipped, and appointed you to do amazing things right where you are—in whatever role you work or serve. Look for those opportunities. Pay attention and seize those moments. At school, at the grocery store, with neighbors, or wherever, you have the opportunity to be the difference in someone's seemingly ordinary day. As Paul said, "Here's what I want you to do, God helping you: Take your everyday, ordinary life—your sleeping, eating, going-to-work, and walking-around life—and place it before God as an offering. Embracing what God does for you is the best thing you can do for him" (Rom. 12:1 MSG).

It's hard to find a reasonable excuse for saying no to traveling hospitality when it doesn't even interfere with your busy schedule . . . because you're already there! For me, it took chiseling the chip off my shoulder, handing my crazy schedule over to Him, and inviting others to join me on my blanket—my new home away from home, my open door out on the open road.

When I first shared this book's title, *Just Open the Door*, with my mom, I explained that the door is also a metaphor. It doesn't always mean our home. As cheesy as it sounds, we can ask the Lord to open the door and soften our hearts to reveal needs around us. It may mean opening our car door to offer someone a ride, or opening the local coffee-shop door to share a few minutes of conversation—anywhere God has planted us for a season, or even for a thirty-minute lag between other appointments. My mom took this challenge seriously and a few weeks later reported back.

"Jen, that concept has opened my eyes. I've had so many opportunities to welcome people into my life that I normally walk right on by." At the gym, for example, a woman happened to mention to her that she was having a tough day. So, thinking of this as her open door, my mom probed a bit more, and the lady opened up about some of the struggles she was confronting. They bonded enough in those few moments to exchange phone numbers and over the course of the week had multiple conversations where my mom served as a source of encouragement.

I've tried to both model and discuss this concept with our children too. Our daughter serves on her eighth-grade church leadership team. As we were chitchatting on her bed last Sunday, she remarked, "Mom, I love being on it because I get to talk to so many new people."

I pointed to the sign hanging above her bed that reads, "Someday I will change the world." I said, "Honey, not 'someday.' Changing the world starts today. I'm glad being on the leadership team gives you a natural opening for it—and it's so great you're doing that—but you can be the difference for one person every day, anywhere. Purpose in your heart to seek them out. Find the girl sitting by herself. The girl that seems disconnected and lonely. You can make a difference right now."

See, the Lord has given us everything we need to walk this road of welcome. I can do it. My mom can do it. My daughter can do it. *You* can do it. It's not only a special gift for outgoing personalities or the good conversationalist. There's nothing you must do or change about yourself before you begin. Offering a warm welcome isn't about perception, personality, or even productivity. It's about starting exactly with how God made you, right where He's put you, right now. And if ever you begin to worry it's not something you can do, remind yourself what *He* can do and how much He believes in you. If He can hold the stars in the sky, He can hold your anxious heart in the palm of his hand. "He who calls you is faithful" (1 Thess. 5:24).

God wasn't trying to pull a "gotcha" moment when He commanded us to pursue hospitality. God's Word is true, so He knows exactly what He's doing. He has full confidence that you can accomplish what He's called you forth to do. No questions asked.

It's been sixteen years since that first season of football, and one of our family's most significant spheres of influence for the kingdom of God has come from taking our hospitality on the road. I've brought hospitality to playgrounds and parks, to fields and forests, but mostly to hundreds of games for varying sports. I've hosted brunches for the team while squeezed in hotel rooms and organized potlucks in more gyms than I care to count. I've done "church" in the stands while moms have cried over overwhelming circumstances, and I've seen God show up in mighty ways, simply by saying yes to walking a road of welcome. It begins with simple, steadfast steps of surrender, and often our smallest steps, repeated over time, hold the most significance.

As you go about today's activities, love your neighbor as yourself at the bank, on the football field, at your grocery store, and anywhere your daily grind takes you. Extend a longer "blanket" because you never know what might happen when you offer up your own version of Goldfish crackers and applesauce to those around you.

One invitation may change a generation.

I'll never forget my mom's simple declaration to me when I was fifteen. "Honey, with summer break beginning, I've signed you up as a weekly volunteer at the nursing home."

You did what? I didn't say it, but I thought it. Dread, discomfort, and nerves set in. This was not how I envisioned my summer break. Yet my mom knew her high school daughter and knew what I needed more than I needed television and endless free time.

My mom was (and is) a studier of my spirit—a wonderful lesson I've gleaned from her and applied with my own children. By stripping away my comfort zone and cracking open the door to a God-sized appointment, she knew my selfish heart would soften.

It took two weeks for me to get past the bad attitude. Two weeks of complaining, two weeks of discomfort, and two weeks spent attempting to change my mom's mind (sorry, mom), but then it happened: a whole new world opened for me. A self-absorbed high schooler crossed generational lines and experienced fully what Psalm 78 talks about, the "things we have heard and known and that our fathers have passed down to us" (v. 3). I sat at the feet of wisdom and soaked in stories that breathed of lives well spent, as well as desperate cries from those whose paths held soul-wrenching regret, who longed for a do-over.

It's as if the Holy Spirit whispered, "Listen up, young thing. Open your heart to what I have in store for you this summer. Tear off the blinders and learn from the past generations. Heed their words, share their stories, and remember."

I remember all right. I remember the hard mixture of smells—of sickness and fragility and disinfectant and lots of sweet, soft perfumes and tobacco. I remember the juxtaposition of sounds—of love and laughter from a grandchild's rare visit, hidden amid cries and cursing during physical therapy. Those sensory memories never quite leave you.

But more importantly, I remember the transforming power of their life stories. Stories that opened a door through which He boldly stepped and carved a new path. Stories of chivalry and war-torn loves. Stories of sacrifice through service. Stories of loneliness and loss, of burying both child and spouse. All summer long I soaked up sentiments shared by generations who had gone before, wisdom weathered through decades of life and death—gleaned from people who could never accept an invitation to come to the house but who could be part of my life if I'd only go to theirs.

That summer marked me. A fifteen-year-old old soul, never to be the same again. In fact, it marked me enough that I carried this deeply entrenched experience into my own mothering. I yearned for our children to have a multigenerational love for those around them because for the most part our society doesn't think this way. Schools, churches, sometimes even whole neighborhoods are built around age segregation. That's why as a parent I've realized I must be purposeful in bridging the generational gap. As a former high school youth director, I knew how many students graduate without any meaningful relationships with the older generations. And I believed (and still believe) that in the hustle and bustle of daily life and doing good, as well in our relentless quest for staying culturally relevant, we can easily and foolishly deem the wisdom of past generations irrelevant. We can lose our heritage. We can miss out on the generational legacy waiting to be shared.

So for years I took our kids to the nursing home, a perfect place to share your hospitality. (But please, don't only show up for Christmas caroling. Retirement homes are overrun with "feel-good" holiday visitors who never return the rest of the year. Remember . . . they're people, not a project.) We made crafts with the residents and sang songs with them. But mainly we listened, even while wiping drooling mouths and cleaning up spilled drinks. My children understood it was okay if someone fell asleep in the middle of a conversation. And they learned to hold Miss Daisy's hands real tight even when her arm started shaking uncontrollably because she loved the feel of their soft skin on hers. Unlike me, they were exposed to these dynamics at an early enough age so they never developed an awkwardness around their elders. Being around older people was just what they knew, and even now they can walk into the most uncomfortable situations like nobody's business.

Those years were precious—their love unconditional, developing sensitivities that can only be caught, not taught. They graduated from crafts to gardening, to cleaning, to mowing, and even to eating at Bojangles with their favorite "Uncle Bill," a neighbor down the street with whom they shared life ever since they were little.

Uncle Bill would pick them up every week, and they'd spend the morning sitting in the back of our country store gas station—my teen daughter, my nephew, and a slew of seventy- and eighty-year-old men shooting the breeze. Can you even imagine? It was a regular *Andy Griffith* episode. When Uncle Bill died last year, a piece of shared generational legacy died with him. But they've tucked their memories along with the lessons learned close to their hearts, ready to pull them out and use them again as a model for others.

I believe this warms the heart of God to see His children (you and me, as well as your and my children) pursuing the on-the-go hospitality modeled by Jesus. As we throw aside our comfortable excuses and offer up our blanket or our seat on the bleachers, He brings people within range who need what He's equipped us to share. Don't underestimate the impact. As we imagine our door becoming a portable invitation, able to be extended like a traveling word of welcome, He allows its hinges to swing open in places all over town, even all over the world. As we bring our hospitality on the road, it can also take us into *other* people's homes, those who could or would never come to us.

And we're only getting started with the endless possibilities of where our hospitality can go. As you get in your car today remember—Hospitality: will Travel.

Isn't that what Jesus said? And did? And asked us to do?

"To go"?

Dear Jen

I love this concept of shifting hospitality from something that only happens in my home to living a life of welcome everywhere I go. Do you have any practical suggestions for something I can do with ladies at my office? Most of us eat at our desks and don't socialize very much.

Working Hard

Dear WH,

During warmer months, why not host your own "Garden Luncheon" during your break? Find a picnic table, shelter, or gazebo at a local park and make it special.

Arrive early, add a tablecloth, a vase with fresh flowers, light a few candles, pour drinks in long-stemmed water glasses, and bring glass plates or use pretty disposable ones. Purchase some chicken croissant sandwiches, fruit, and a few cookies at the local grocery store, and treat your coworkers to a lunch to remember. They'll be moved that you cared enough to shower them with your time.

If something outdoors isn't an option, invite them to your desk for brownies or mimic a garden party in the break room. Sweet treat invitations always break the ice and can be a stepping stone for a new lunchtime tradition.

Jen

Elevate the Ordinary

❀ Create your own "Hospitality on the Go" party box. I purchase inexpensive candleholders, tablecloths, Mason jars, or any kind of unique party décor at the thrift store or when they're on sale. I store them in a large Rubbermaid bin that I've dubbed the Party Box. My one box has now stretched to multiple boxes, but everyone knows I'm their girl for dressing up a drab spot in minutes. I enjoy sharing this with others, and my box has helped decorate receptions, showers, parties, conferences, end-of-year banquets, and more.

❀ When you're intentional about buying items "off season" and on sale, then you don't have the pressure or expense of paying full price during the planning process. After holidays, buy items that aren't holiday specific for 50–75 percent off. Pastel Easter colors can be used for women's gatherings. Silver and gold Christmas items, as well as Hanukkah's traditional white, silver, and blue colors are perfect for any occasion throughout the year.

EXTRA
HELPING *from my brother Scott*

Your House Is My House

A quick round of word association with *hospitality* would likely invoke tones of "welcoming," "hosting," "entertaining," and "inviting." Perhaps *mi casa es su casa* (my house is your house) best embodies the open-door-invitation attitude.

However, need it be *mi casa*? My suggested twist is that the essence of hospitality stems from my spiritual heart, not my physical home.

Why is this distinction important? Because many people will never venture into my home, especially those in the older generation who remember (and miss) the time when front-porch hospitality was the norm. For example, our home is not handicap accessible, which many older friends require. And it's no small commute from their house to ours, which is inconvenient for daylight-only drivers. How, then, can my parents or other seniors enjoy my hospitality?

Practicality dictates that *my* hospitality must be demonstrated in *their* house, akin to churches ministering to shut-ins. My house can't travel to them, but my heart can.

Indeed, that sounds awkward. It hints of showing up uninvited and imparting pressure on others to assume the host role. Though some relationships afford the flexibility to swing by at any time, this is not the norm, and we don't always have a convenient excuse. How then can we get our foot in their door to extend sincere and intentional hospitality? Here are a few ideas:

- Offer to swing by with flowers from the garden or home-baked goodies.
- Ask if you can visit to get their help or advice. This strategy is far from contrived; it shouldn't take much thinking to generate significant ways you can learn from their wisdom and skill set. I'm now a beekeeper thanks to my elderly neighbor.

- Tell them you'd love to hear about their childhood, military experiences, what the town used to be like, etc. By imparting value to their lives via attentive listening, you're validating them in a powerful way.

My buddy Mark is a prime example of offering this kind of hospitality on the go. I only wish I had been the one who'd had the vision and initiative to pull this off, but at least I was wise enough to make it a priority on my calendar.

Mark asked our nonagenarian neighbor, an older gentleman named Hillary, if he could host a party at his house because he knew our ninety-two-year-old neighbor wouldn't come to him. The premise was that he needed his large workshop area for the guys to gather in, and he promised to do all the work.

Given the nod, he invited about twenty others, including several of Hillary's friends. (They may not have attended something at Mark's house, but they were comfortable going to Hillary's.) The invite boasted a menu of grilled round steak, baked potato, garden greens, mixed drinks, and dessert. Attendees ranged from their twenties to their nineties; it was an awesome cross-generational mix.

Once we arrived, we expanded on the menu details:

- "Grilled round steak" was bologna slices tossed into a cast-iron skillet atop the blazing Franklin stove.
- The "baked potato" description conveniently omitted the word "chips."
- The "garden greens" could be torn from a head of lettuce and added to the bologna sandwiches.
- The beverage cans in the ice bucket consisted of a "mix" of Pepsi, Sprite, and root beer.
- Oreos rounded out our "dessert."

And for the entertainment? Small clusters of mingling evolved into the nightcap game of "Two Truths and a Lie." No comedy club in town could have replicated the belly laughs, as this diverse crowd shared adventure after hilarious adventure.

Oh, what a night was had by all! And how easy it would be to duplicate such an outreach. Simple. Cheap. Nonthreatening. Instead of opening his home in hospitality, Mark took his hospitality not only to Hillary but to Hillary's friends as well.

Hospitality doesn't always take place in our homes, and sometimes it may be more effective and practical when taken to the homes of others—seniors or not. Who's with me in taking our hospitality on the road?

5

Everyday Moments

"I've never seen anything quite like this, Jennifer," the golf pro remarked as he gestured around our kitchen.

My eyes followed his, scanning the room closely, stumped about what he meant. Nothing looked out of the ordinary, though my tummy did tweak a bit wondering what he noticed that I'd missed. With me, it could be a multitude of things.

Simple foods lined the kitchen counter alongside bags of chips and spilled popcorn. Black Sharpie markers surrounded the sea of empty red Solo cups. Teen boys from the local public high school golf team sat on the couch; a few others were tossing around the football outside. Victorious shouts echoed from another mini corn hole tournament, while moms balanced paper plates on their laps, reporting the latest school happenings. My next-door neighbor nephews crowded the island looking for lukewarm leftovers. The athletic director and his wife were nearby too, recounting memorable student tales from years past as my patient husband asked engaging questions.

I continued examining our home. While incredibly noisy and filled with activity, I didn't see anything too out of hand yet unfortunately nothing very remarkable either. In fact, if he'd known my impressive plans for this get-together celebrating our son's golf team and how they'd all been ditched by the wayside, he'd realize what he was actually witnessing was a disaster.

I'd bought supplies to create the most amazing golf-hole centerpiece for the table, adapting blue tissue paper to mimic the water hazard and sand for the trap. Oh, and the cake—green food coloring to turn shredded coconut into grass, and a little flag to mark the hole in one. Yep, I executed it perfectly. But only in my mind. I never even got around to buying the coach's gift because, well . . . because life happened. A series of unexpected obligations arose the day before, and so my detailed potluck list sat incomplete, leaving me twenty steps behind. The grand décor theme never materialized, so I blew up a few balloons, dangled them from our kitchen light fixture with masking tape, embraced an "it is what it is" mentality, and called it a day. From my vantage point it was the most ordinary, unexceptional gathering I'd ever hosted. I almost hoped for a return of the tornado warning party to liven things up and give guests something to talk about. (Almost.)

And yet he couldn't stop commenting on it. On how special it was. "I've never seen anything quite like this, Jennifer—your family, the love here. Such joy comes from your home. I feel love all around. It's truly remarkable."

"Thank you so much," I said, stammering something about the Lord's graciousness and how we're a continuous work in progress. Everything in me really wanted to apologize for my lack of preparation, the messy house, and the store-bought food. The only reason I stopped myself was because of a spiritual truth I've come to believe: how apologizing in response to others' kind words robs the Lord of His due glory and subtly attempts to turn the focus back to me. And it wasn't about me.

But as I let his words marinate, my tentative spirit shifted to joyful confirmation—this is exactly why our family opens the door.

Paul's encouragement to "take every opportunity to open our life and home to others" (Rom. 12:13 VOICE) feels daunting to even attempt in real life. "Every opportunity"—how is that even possible?

But here's where we need *another* perspective change . . . because he didn't first clarify this challenge with a list of expectations. Nowhere can I find in the Bible, "Love others well, but not until you've mastered ten tips for hosting a beautifully organized dinner party." We aren't given any qualifications about the size of our home or the ingredients necessary for a culinary delight. Instead, we're repeatedly told in Scripture that the Lord chooses to receive and multiply the smallest offerings we have to give.

So isn't it just like Him to show up so unexpectedly and use a simple gathering like my hastily thrown-together team party to showcase His beauty amid our ordinary evening? He is so good and gracious like that. He doesn't require or expect anything fancy; we put that pressure on ourselves. He delights in the everyday average.

Whatever your everyday average happens to be.

As a young mom with many little ones underfoot, the monotony of my hours often closed in on me. Everything was so daily. So seemingly insignificant. Do they really have to eat again? Didn't I just make lunch? Success on some days meant I'd been able to bribe one of them to finish a banana and the diapers hadn't run out. Gold-star moments consisted of nailing the three biggies—food, clothing, and shelter—thinking even these minor accomplishments deserved celebration. (If you need a mom star, come find me. I think I'll start carrying them in my purse.)

Only on rare and isolated days did I get both a quiet time and a shower in before noon, but if I managed to meet a work deadline and restart (again) the still-damp laundry from the day before, I felt like Wonder Woman. When I attempted some semblance of structured learning time, grocery shopped with all of our little ones, and served a hot dinner, typically without a meltdown, I basically hurdled tall buildings in a single bound. And if that's you today, mom, I'm pausing to commemorate. You go, girl. You're someone who will understand better than most the realization that came to me during those years. If Jesus said to "love your neighbor," well . . . my closest neighbors looked a whole lot like our kids, glued to my hip being all neighborly like. So I guess that's biblical.

But somewhere in between the monotonous and the heroic days, restlessness seeped into my soul. I became antsy. My everyday wasn't enough. I started listening to others questioning why I wasn't doing something special with the gifts God had given me, and I measured my moments by their moving marker. Rumbles of personal discontent and feelings of insignificance began stirring, and I wondered if there wasn't more for me than this constant cycle of meals, diapers, tantrums

(I've quit these for the most part), and occasional field trips alone to the grocery store.

During that time, my husband gifted me with a pivotal weekend away to sit under the teaching of a Christian mentor of mine I'd never met, Elisabeth Elliot. I often think about that conference. With her gracious yet challenging demeanor, she began by cutting straight to the heart of Jesus' call to discipleship. In the moment I tried to scribble everything down, and decades later I'm reading that messy scrawl from my journal. "Do you want to be His disciple? You don't have to," she reminded us, "but to love Him is bound with sacrifice. To answer yes is to suffer, to deny yourself, and to really mean 'Lord, do anything with me You want.'"

This woman knew all too well what it meant to suffer. Widowed after her husband, Jim, was killed on the mission field, she became a single mother who chose to forgive and continue ministering to the same tribe who'd committed the murder, loving them and pursuing community with them. Who does that? It's unheard of. She practiced hospitality by welcoming her enemies into her life, her home, her everyday moments.

I sat there astounded, trying to imagine what I had to offer that was even within the same zip code of sacrifice and servanthood she'd embodied. I'd come grumbling about my first-world problems: messy house, dented minivan, and my nonexistent social life. I'd become discontented because my small moments didn't yield much room for doing bigger, better, bolder acts for Jesus. As she spoke, my heart cried, "Yes, I want to follow You, Lord. Use me," but my mind hesitated. "What does that really look like? How brave do I have to be?"

That's when she uttered a few words that landed on me like a grace balm for my floundering soul: "For me, taking up my cross daily included terrible suffering. For you, your suffering may be in the form of doing small duties that are distasteful to you. It may be having what you don't want or wanting what you don't have. That may be your cross today."

Small duties that are distasteful to me? Wanting what I don't have? My cross today might really look like small, day-in and day-out choices that no one sees, knows, or appreciates? How could she have understood the exact words I needed to hear? She didn't insinuate some sliding scale of spiritual sacrifice. She didn't minimize my feelings of inadequacy because of my "less than" offering. Nor did she elevate what the Lord had required of her to a super-sized status. Whatever I'd been given to do for that day—whatever my everyday entailed—the call was to lay it at the feet of Jesus, a day-to-day surrendering.

I had been set free!

From then on, through God's power, I began to unveil the sacred amid the simple, viewing my series of small, daily moments as a "Gateway to Joy" (to borrow the name of her long-running radio broadcast). I unearthed hidden wonder buried underneath mounds of dirty laundry alongside stray Doritos. Smudged fingerprints revealed masterpieces crafted by my favorite tiny hands. Pulling weeds reminded me of the importance to nurture and fortify the soil of our hearts, while sibling squabbles prompted opportunities for peaceful reconciliation (after much mom-time mediation). The hard work and sacrifices I was making at home with my family were suddenly filled with newfound spiritual significance for me. My tiny, unseen moments mattered. He saw them. He knew. The everyday was my opportunity to serve Him, by serving them. Loving Him and loving them.

But it was also my way to serve others: to seek out their unseen moments and encourage them. With eyes wide open, I now viewed everyday interactions through a new lens, one that widened as needs presented themselves. Whether sitting at a boardroom table, standing in line at the grocery store, or purposely choosing the same bank line to encourage repeated conversations with my teller, the Lord shifted my mind-set from one of irritated interruptions to that of initiating invitation. I pressed into my circumstances around me, took that next step, and marked mundane moments as treasured offerings, pursuing hospitality with purposeful intention. While folding laundry, for instance, I welcomed friends to join me. Instead of struggling solo with dinner ideas, I invited women over to prep main dishes together, conquering each of our mealtime mountains for the week. Frustrated with the baby weight I couldn't shake, friends and I started walking, talking, and pushing our strollers side by side instead of sitting in isolation.

I found His extravagant love laced throughout these little moments. Discovering the fullness of my everyday life truly changed me.

But as I searched Scripture for the varying roles hospitality played, I repeatedly witnessed three main purposes: encouragement to other believers, discipleship, and evangelism.

Well, the relationships I was developing with these other moms, helping one another juggle our parenting responsibilities and live with shared perspective—this qualified as encouraging other believers. And the daily interactions with my children were real-life discipleship venues, trying to model God's heart to them while also teaching them His Word and ways.

But evangelism? My invitations weren't really lining up with that purpose. Unconsciously, I'd created my community within a small Christian bubble. Has this ever happened to you? I attended church, served in a ministry directed at other believers, worked with Christians, hosted a small group for other Christ followers, grabbed coffee with Sunday school friends, and opened the door to play groups consisting of like-minded women. It was a continuous circle of loving on and ministering to those who already knew the answer to the gospel message I desired to share. How had I insulated myself like this? It was not okay. Tentatively, then, I launched a new prayer: "Lord, increase my circle of influence to include those vastly different than me."

And wouldn't you know it, my everyday life provided the perfect opening for God's answer to this prayer as well.

When you live in the South, a lot of great things stem from meals at Chick-fil-A. And one Tuesday as we were there, my four rug rats and I had the play area to ourselves, so I gave them permission to expend as much energy as they wanted while I closed my eyes to enjoy a few moments of spa-like relief. Well, minus the spa and minus the relief, so maybe I just enjoyed a few hands-free moments.

A few other families entered, and as they began their conversation, I couldn't help but hear one of the moms mention how they'd recently "moved to the country." My ears always perk up when country living is mentioned, so I was curious. She commented how everything was a long drive for her and how even this fast-food play land was super far from her house.

Should I barge into their discussion and ask where she lives? I thought. Ack! No, that seemed so awkward. But I kept getting this little nudge pushing me to interject myself. I mean, I'd been praying that my circle might expand, but I didn't think the Holy Spirit would choose for me a stranger at Chick-fil-A . . . or would He?

At this point my internal dialogue started playing hot potato. *Do I walk over there? Will I look like a stalker? When should I jump into the conversation? She's getting a drink refill. Oh bummer, I missed my chance.* Glued to my seat, with my own voice bouncing back and forth in my mind, I couldn't seem to make a move. *Seriously, what's the chance she lives anywhere near me anyway? Highly unlikely.* We live in such a tiny Podunk town; I use a different city name when people ask my address because they'd never know what I was talking about otherwise. *Let's stop this tug-of-war. Let's call playtime to a halt, gather the kids, and head for the exit, get out of here.*

The next voice I heard, however, sounded a lot more like the Holy Spirit: "Jen, did you really mean what you prayed? Or was it lip service offered up for your checklist? Remember when I asked you not to forget to show hospitality to strangers? Are you going to love bravely?" Ouch! He was right. He'd presented this moment, and now I had a choice to make. I could courageously step out of my comfort zone and become the host I desired, or I could be held hostage by others' opinions of me, by my fear of failure or the risk of rejection.

I chiseled off the glue and walked over to their table. My heart raced, my face flushed. I even felt actual sweat dripping between my bra. But I continued on.

"Hi, ladies. I didn't mean to eavesdrop, but it's hard to keep from it in here." (insert nervous laughter) "You mentioned moving out to the country. I know it's a long shot, but I live in the country too. Can I ask where you moved to?"

There, I'd blurted it out. I waited.

Those few seconds seemed to stretch like hours before she responded, "You probably aren't familiar with the area. It's super far away."

"Probably not, but give me a try."

Right then, I'm pretty sure the Lord chuckled as she responded with the name of our little town! Stunned, my jaw dropped. "No way. That's where I live! Where exactly?" (Cue the angels high-fiving up in heaven as they enjoyed watching this unfold.)

Turns out, she lived three miles from our house, which—for you city folk, "three miles" in country terms means we may as well have been sharing a driveway. That's next-door neighbor material. I still can't believe it. We exchanged numbers, and within days I'd invited her and her daughter over for lunch.

What if I'd let doubt defeat me? What if I hadn't introduced myself? What if I hadn't been praying for a heightened alertness to everyday interactions? Think of the blessing I'd have missed out on: loving on a special woman whom I've come to adore.

Over and over I witness divine appointments forged among the ordinary. Day by day I try pressing into things that don't garner any applause but allow me to invest in seemingly average moments. It's in these small, everyday choices when I become more and more like Him and less and less like myself. As I toss the salad and set the table, I feel His pleasure. When I stumble through the dark to comfort a feverish child, He is near. As I clear my busy calendar to hold my scared friend's hand, I sense His presence.

"Do not forget to show hospitality to strangers, for by so doing some people have shown hospitality to angels without knowing it" (Heb. 13:2 NIV). When we plant ourselves in small-moment living, we can't help but be transformed by our great big God.

One everyday at a time.

As I think back on my unimpressive golf gathering—and yet how much it impressed one of our guests—I realize again the simple beauty of opening my ordinary door in obedience and creating space to allow God to do something pretty miraculous with it. It's crazy humbling really because it felt like I didn't do enough, but as Oswald Chambers says, "We always know when Jesus is at work because He produces in the commonplace something that is inspiring."[5]

What amazes me more is what we as believers have allowed to be stolen from us, right out from under our noses. Why are we searching for something more? Do you remember how basic this evening was? There was nothing earth-shattering about it (red Solo cups for the win). So, how could something as simple as opening the doors of our everyday life become surprising enough to appear starkly countercultural to people? As if they've never seen anything like it before. It goes back to that swinging door—*slam, slam*—the sweetness in community is found in the simplicity of the ordinary. God makes it so easy to find. It's already right here in front of you. Ready to use, ready to offer up as a sacrifice for His glory.

So throw that party for no reason. Crank the music, pass the chips and salsa, and celebrate your everyday moments. I'm convinced that if we live out our ordinary moments as if they result in changed lives, our faithful legacy will shape generations.

He loves to make use of it all.

Dear Jen

Why do you think that ordinary evening stood out so much to your guests? What specific things did you do to be intentional with that time?

Curious

Dear Curious,

Besides always serving lots of food, we incorporate a few additional elements that seem commonplace since we do them at most get-togethers, but for many it's revolutionary.

1. *Greeting.* Go above and beyond with welcoming guests, making them feel included and loved. Greetings were significant in the New Testament letters, so I take them as a cue. Every person, even the shy woman who rarely speaks, has a precious story. When she walks through our door, I want her to know she's seen, valued, and matters.

2. *Time of blessing over guests.* As hosts we have a unique opportunity to impart words of great influence over those in our home. Proverbs 18:21 reminds us that "death and life are in the power of the tongue," and we take every chance possible to speak words of life and encouragement to our guests. Each situation will be different based on the guest list, but taking the time to shower gratitude, to uplift, to bring hope, and—on this specific night—even to challenge guests can profoundly affect people. Don't take for granted the impact of life-giving words. I believe those words of blessing my husband spoke over the coaches, parents, and staff marked them in a powerful way.

3. *Circle of prayer.* Since we were already circled up for the time of blessing, my husband took a minute to explain that our circle represents continuous, unconditional love. Those few sentences made known whose house ours represents, and then he prayed for those gathered. For those not accustomed to corporate prayer, I've been amazed at how many people have mentioned our tradition of circling up.

4. *Open heart, open home equals flexibility.* Throughout the night, people were in and out of our house. So many moments could have allowed stress to drive my emotions, but the more we relax, release control, and enjoy our guests, the more we engage their hearts.

Jen

Elevate the Ordinary

❀ Stimulating the senses is a wonderful way we experience life and communicate love in simple ways. Our senses hold strong triggers. We can taste a favorite meal, and instantly we're back in grandma's kitchen. Think through each of your five senses, and identify ways you can engage your senses this week in your home. Here are a few ideas.

❀ *Smell.* Open the windows. Simmer apple peels with cinnamon on the stove. Bake bread. Diffuse essential oils or light a scented candle. Start your Crock-Pot before work so you can enjoy the aroma when you walk in the house.

❀ *Sight.* Hang Scripture and art that points to Him. When people enter your home, it leaves no doubt of what's most important in your family. Fill a pretty bowl with colorful fruit, or fill a Mason jar with fresh-cut flowers, foliage, or flowering twigs or branches from outside. Print a new family picture and display it proudly.

❀ *Touch.* Greet family with a big hug and kiss. It's okay to go over the top with your kids. Surprise them with a new way to tuck them in at night. Lay your hands on them and pray a blessing over them. Even our big boys need to know how much their momma loves them.

❀ *Sound.* What is your tone? We are the thermostat in our homes, and we set the temperature for our family and friends. For one day, practice the art of whispering to your children. You'll be amazed at what happens. Play peaceful music or praise songs in the background. Find songs that help you—and them—memorize Scripture.

❀ *Taste.* Surprise your family with their favorite meal or dessert. Make today a "just because I love you" day, and tuck love notes with favorite snacks in their bed, backpack, car seat, etc. Recreate an old family recipe, and share the story behind why it's meaningful.

6

Who Are My Neighbors?

"Mom, we've invited all the neighbors," my five-year-old son told me as I chopped veggies for dinner. "They're coming tonight for our basketball game."

"What are you talking about? What basketball game?" I inquired, knowing we didn't really know our neighbors well, and we sure didn't have a place for a basketball game.

"Yep, remember yesterday when I told you we were working on a project? Well, we made up official Tar Heels tickets, drew up invitations, and then walked to all the neighbors' houses, inviting them to our cool game tonight. We have it all planned. The invitations say, 'North Carolina Tar Heels vs. The World.' The four of us are the Tar Heels (my two sons plus their two cousins), and Jimmy (the oldest cousin/brother) is The World since he's the oldest and says he can take us all easily."

"Who made up the invitations?" I asked, thinking these young guns surely couldn't have pulled this off by themselves.

"Well, Jimmy and Leah helped us write the invitations out, but we made all the tickets and then walked door-to-door inviting everyone. A bunch of people promised us they were coming."

And there it was. An open and unassuming door to every neighbor on our street, using some of the most unlikely instruments of all. I'm pretty sure a roomful of grownups, strategizing for months to determine who would be best suited for spurring social and gospel change in our immediate zip code, would never have come up with these two: our preschool sons. I think the theme of 1 Timothy 4:12 is pretty appropriate here: *Do not look down on anyone because they're young.* Wow, I underestimated the potential of focus and determination.

Once again I was reminded how we overthink hospitality. I didn't do a thing to invite our neighbors. I didn't worry about cleaning the house or entertaining them. I didn't even have to provide any snacks because our young boys had thought it all through. They filled brown paper bags with popcorn, poured lemonade in plastic cups, had faith that those they'd invited would come, and prepared accordingly.

I'll be honest, my nervous momma's heart was afraid they might have put all this hard work into their "worldwide" event and no one would show up. But hours later as game time approached, ten neighbors trudged past our house and through our weedy lawn to the "basketball court." (The reason I add the quotes is because the "court" is an old hunk of leftover cement we'd dumped in the woods. It's definitely not a place I'd send any adult on our property, so it's a good thing they didn't ask me.)

The kids directed them first to the "box office"—a card table set up with appropriate signage, which doubled as a concession stand for handing out free drinks and snacks. Then all the fans took their seats on bleachers built out of milk cartons and long boards, just in time for tip-off.

I won't go into details of the game action, since a few questionable fouls were still being appealed for several weeks afterward. What I *can* tell you is that while the kids were smiling ear to ear the whole time, I think our neighbors were the ones who enjoyed it even more. Amid a crowd consisting of a variety of ages and backgrounds, we made some precious new friends that day . . . all because of the audacious plan of some little kids with even bigger hearts.

Kids make it seem so easy, don't they?

They always have. My husband grew up in Green Bay, Wisconsin, where his neighborhood created the fabric of their social community. Their entire street lived interconnected with one another, caring and looking out for one another. Neighbor kids gathered every day after school for wannabe Packers games and stickball in the street.

"Summer evening basketball games started every night at ten," my husband tells me. "If someone didn't show up, we'd come find them. Then when the game finished, all of us would move inside to watch *M*A*S*H* reruns."

"Every night?" I asked him.

"Yep, like clockwork. Remember, these were the days before anyone could DVR a show or be distracted with social media," he reminded me. If you lived in that neighborhood, you were one of the gang. Everyone belonged. Varying personalities didn't matter. If problems arose, the kids worked through it like a family (or, should I add, like a functional one). The kids on his street became lifelong best friends. In fact, when the two of us started dating, he still lived on that same tiny street. While some of the neighbors had come and gone, many chose to stay rooted and connected. Even as their careers escalated and they could afford bigger houses, they chose to stay put, content to uphold and engage the unique neighboring community they'd grown to love.

Sounds pretty special, doesn't it? Not many of us had that same experience, and a lot fewer experience it now. But isn't that the kind of community you'd like for your children? Isn't that the kind of community you'd like to foster around yourself?

As with many aspects of hospitality, we've dismissed an entire culture of neighboring well, until now the relational distance between neighbors has reached an epidemic level. Neighbors simply don't know one another as they did in years past. In fact, in a distinct generational flip-flop from the 1970s, when neighbors hung out at least twice a week, one-third of all Americans today have never interacted with any of their neighbors. Ever! More than half of us don't even know our neighbors' names, let alone have a relationship with them. And even among those who do know their neighbors a little, who talk to them once in a while, nearly all of them (when asked) say they've never had any "meaningful interaction" with a neighbor. It's almost nonexistent.[6]

So we have a choice to make. It doesn't have to be this way. But if we want it to be different, if we want anything approaching what my husband enjoyed in the neighborhood of his youth—and more importantly, if we want to engage community with the love of God among the people who share city blocks and other living spaces with us—it does take an intentional, purposeful decision to help usher in a change for our neighborhoods.

I absolutely love to hear stories of neighborhoods doing it right, creating the kinds of places where we all want to live . . . where spontaneous parades put on by bored kids lead to community occurring in the street. Where lemonade stands pop up on a street corner and neighbors stop to support the budding entrepreneur. Where grills are pulled into a cul-de-sac for a weekend barbecue, or where an apartment complex hosts a potluck in their clubhouse.

These aren't *Leave It to Beaver* fantasies that are impossible to reestablish. Simple steps can change the way we do community with those who live in closest proximity to us. Little decisions can reveal the great needs waiting out there, crying to be met, as we open our literal door. To befriend. To be a light in the darkness.

We've already looked at the Great Commandment: loving God and loving our neighbor as ourselves. But rethink it in terms of proximity, in terms of our actual, literal neighbors. Begin with the ones who live next door, those people with whom we're too embarrassed to initiate conversation because we can't remember their names. Or how about the couple who recently moved in across the street, the ones we've avoided ever since our trash can rolled into their yard and they got upset about the mess. Maybe it's the neighbor who shares the apartment wall, whose loud noise brings constant annoyance.

What does it mean to really love our neighbors? Not with an agenda. Not as a project to check off our to-do lists. I realize it might require a heartfelt choice to "fake it till you make it," knowing that the Spirit will stir up love, even when we don't feel it. But this is about cultivating an authentic relationship with people we are commanded to *love*—not necessarily *like*—and then letting God do whatever He desires to do with it from there. My fear is that we've sort of generalized this concept of *neighbor* to the point where we don't even apply it to those people who are our most *obvious* neighbors, the ones we most often see in passing. That's why I'm issuing a call to begin putting this principle into practice right where we live.

As I think through how to love them, I first imagine ways in which I want to be loved. Encouraging words or simple acts of service are always great beginnings to any neighboring relationship.

Start simply. If you notice pieces of trash that have blown into a neighbor's yard, don't walk by them; pick them up. Encourage your kids to do the same. Your neighbor may not realize the simple effort, but it proactively shifts your own thoughts toward others and away from yourself. Carve out time each week to ask, "What tangible needs do I see in my neighborhood, and how can I be part of the solution?"

Put names with faces. How about the neighbor whose name slips your mind? This week make it your priority to watch for a time to connect with her. Take the first step and bridge the disconnect. If it's been months since you've talked, humble yourself. "I'm so sorry I've been too busy and haven't taken the time to get to know you more. I want to change that. I'm so embarrassed, but please remind me of your name again. I'm Jen." Leading with honesty and vulnerability always serves as a bridge builder.

Just pay attention. If neighbors put a lot of work into beautifying their yard, notice it, appreciate it, let them know you recognize their great gift, and ask for some tips on your own yard. Everyone loves to share their knowledge about something they're passionate about. Find out your neighbors' interests and inquire about them. Encourage them. You never know what new skill you might learn.

Make the invitation. If you're grilling out and see a neighbor in the backyard or out on the street, even if you've gone months without talking to them, this is your time for a do-over. "Hey, Janet, I know this is out of the blue, but I bought a bunch of extra burgers we will never be able to eat by ourselves. Would you like to join us on the back deck for some dinner?" This is a casual, nonthreatening invitation to break down a barrier. Even if she says no, you've opened the door to a follow-up conversation.

All of these options serve as simple bridge-building ideas to strengthen neighboring relationships. It doesn't take rocket science, but it does take action.

And it all starts with looking at Jesus' Great Commandment in its most literal sense. Do we live as people who are loved by the Most High God? Are we loving our neighbors in this same way?

Neighboring well doesn't happen by chance; nor does it happen overnight. We have to pursue it. We have to seek out those seemingly insignificant moments where all we're doing is putting love for others at the top of our priority list. Because with time, these moments can shape the framework of our neighborhoods as we model Christ on a day-in and day-out basis.

The fact that the "love thy neighbor" command is made to us in Scripture means it applies to all of us, even to those introverts in the bunch. No matter what our given makeup, we need to shove aside the notion that hospitality is only for people who like big groups, dinner parties, and lingering conversations. There are many creative alternatives for practicing hospitality and showing love to our neighbors that lean into our God-given personalities.

My friend Shellie, for instance, said for years when her neighbors would plan a Bunco night, she'd always use the "I'm sorry, I can't because of the baby" excuse. But when her "baby" turned three, she realized her standard fallback didn't work so well anymore. What does a girl do for an excuse, then, when she's run through all the obvious ones? Come up with new ones? Even if less believable ones?

Or maybe just stop making them.

"Jen, I'm getting there," she told me. "I really am. I know how important community is for all of us," how it's not just a mark of good neighborliness but is actually a beautiful, undeniable expression of faith. "You always remind me to take baby steps," she said. And for her first step? She opened the door and walked to her own backyard, hosting an outdoor movie night with neighborhood families. All she had to do was provide popcorn, soda, and her lawn.

"My husband actually volunteered us without asking," she confessed, "but he forced me to take the first step, and I'm really glad he did." It started a process of helping her overcome the fears that came along with her naturally shy personality.

Shellie admits she's comfortable in groups for only about two or three hours, after which her introvert tendencies start crying out for a breather. But by hosting an event that incorporated some key boundaries—such as ending at a definite finishing time and not making herself solely responsible for carrying on a long conversation—she set herself up for success while stepping into this new life of welcoming others.

I do want to be careful here, though, not to oversell the simplicity of this. I'm not pretending there aren't obstacles to overcome in developing new friendships or that we can always keep tight controls around how it plays out. Remember again what Jesus defined as the mark of a disciple, including the call to deny those desires that cater solely to ourselves. For as we become more comfortable with our geographic neighbors and invite them into our lives, we do open the door to the unexpected.

Like, say, the dreaded drop-in.

Yes, this is terrifying and paralyzes the best of us. Can I see your hand if you've heard the doorbell ring, and your immediate reaction looked like something out of our grade school fire drill, "Stop, drop, and roll"?

We've all done it. And when I asked some of the (in)courage girls, they admitted it.

"Unscheduled knocks at my front door leave my heart dropping into my stomach," Krista said. "My first instinct is to drop to the floor, crawl to the nearest window, peek out the blinds, and make no sudden movements. I've done it. Yes, I have." And, okay, she added, since we're all being honest here, "I've actually yelled to my kids, 'Stay away from the windows!' so no one knows we're at home."

Julie, though complicit by her laughter, said she's actually gotten a little better at the drop-in, less terrified of it. One way she's learned to handle it is by telling her friends, "I'd love for you to pop in, but you need to send me a 'broom and bra' text first—enough time to sweep and get fully dressed." Three cheers for a broom-and-bra text. We definitely need to make that a "thing."

One of my favorite introvert friends confessed, "I can't do drop-ins no matter how much my heart wants to be okay with it because they cause me serious panic attacks." Instead, she's identified how God has wired her and has started a new tradition within her neighborhood group. Whenever she's ready to extend an invitation, she updates her Facebook status spontaneously with, "I'm ready for you. Drop in anytime between 10 and 2." I love that idea! She still welcomes others but doesn't use her personality or her fear of the drop-in as an excuse.

So that's sort of the consensus on the drop-in. Maybe you register with some of those feelings and comments. But I recently started a knock-down, drag-out debate when I posed the following question on social media: "Is it ever acceptable for someone to invite *herself* over?" The responses ranged from "It's never okay. It's rude and selfish" to "Absolutely! Come on over, the more the merrier." This question doesn't have an easy answer. Truly the thought of an unplanned guest strips us to our most vulnerable.

Here's the kicker, though: Jesus modeled the ultimate drop-in. He turned entertaining etiquette upside down in Luke 19:1–10 when He invited Himself right on over to the house of Zacchaeus, the despised tax collector. Yes, He did.

Can you imagine how frantic Zacchaeus's wife must have been when her husband walked in unannounced with this renowned Teacher trailing close behind? It's possible, I guess, their servants had run ahead to warn her but certainly not in time to give her a sufficient broom-and-bra heads-up. Even if they did reach her first, imagine her shock when they also informed her that Zach (to friends like us) had publicly declared he was taking this opportunity to give away a big chunk of their money. How do you think she liked hearing *that*? Perhaps her loaded husband's wealth was the only thing that made his dreaded job worth the contempt she got from their neighbors. Pair this with the panic of hosting Jesus unexpectedly and, yikes, bless her heart. This was not her day.

Yet for some reason, Jesus knew the importance of inviting Himself over (right there in front of everyone, I might add), letting it be known that He wanted to hang with this tax collector, this wee little man hated by anyone with whom he rubbed shoulders. Jesus, though, deemed him worthy of time at the table. Even worth the risk of appearing as an imposition.

What can we learn from this episode about neighboring well—both as host and as guest? Maybe a lot. Instead of merely being willing to open *our* door, do we also need to sometimes walk through it and reach out to people who might not accept our invitation? Should we go to *them* if they'll never venture out to *us*? Hmmm, might need to chew on that one for a while. But in light of what Jesus did, can we still insist, "That's rude—it's always rude to invite ourselves over," when this kind of radical hospitality turned an outcast host into a critical part of the gospel story?

Isn't it crazy how the Scripture can do a number on our logical opinions and assumptions? Because maybe there's an invitation waiting to be received at *every* door, even those we'd never expect.

All right, let's get practical now and do a little homework. I realize the following exercise (which I'm borrowing from *The Art of Neighboring*) holds the possibility of making you squirm, but I'll tell you in advance, absolutely no self-shaming allowed. Personally, this thing convicts me too, because I am the "Queen of Best Intentions," someone who means to do but then doesn't always do the subsequent follow-through. So, if for no one else, I've accepted this challenge myself, wanting to love my neighbors on purpose in order to (as the book says) "move the Great Commission from a theory into a real-world context."[7] This is about closing the loop on best intentions and making them a reality.

Remember, I can't see your chart. No one's comparing. In my family everything becomes a competition, but rest assured, we are neither keeping score nor giving points. Unless you're my boys. In which case, no promises.

Here we go then. Draw a big square with four lines horizontally and four lines vertically to create nine squares. Put a symbol for your house in the middle square. Then in each of the eight remaining squares, put three lines (a, b, c) one above the other. The eight squares containing the three blank lines represent the eight neighbors who live closest to you.

When I first did this exercise, I started making excuses because we live in the country . . . and because our closest neighbors are twelve acres apart . . . and because it's so easy to make excuses, excuses, excuses . . . until I told myself, like I tell the kids, "Excuses are like armpits; everyone has them." (Not very sophisticated, I know, but it's a great mom visual.) So are you hearing me? *Don't make excuses.*

Maybe your first excuse is, "Hey, I don't even *have* a neighborhood." Then expand your vision. Use the grid for the people at work or another place where you spend a lot of time. Adjust it to your setting. This is about getting to know those in your closest sphere of influence, so there's no right or wrong answer.

Do you recall how I mentioned that half of us don't know our neighbors' names? If we're going to love them well, remembering their names is a pretty good place to start. So, as you go around your grid, complete the following steps:

- On the first line (a), jot down as many of your neighbors' names as you know. You may be one of the people I sense freaking out right now, wondering if the name of your neighbor's dog counts. (No—although walking your dog is an excellent way to meet your neighbors and also get in shape.)
- For the second line (b), write a few facts or relevant pieces of information that have come from an actual conversation

between yourself and the person/family whose names you've written in the box. Again, "They have a grey cat who uses our sandbox as a litter box" does not count. These should be facts such as occupation, where they grew up, hobbies, etc.

- On the third line (c), write something that's even more specific and meaningful about them—information that would only come after having connected with them on a more personal level such as their dreams, celebrations, struggles, issues with children, or church history.

Be brutally honest with yourself as you fill out this chart. Don't write things down just to minimize your guilt. To love your neighbor better begins with understanding how you've done it in the past. Let this be a step toward truly growing in connection with your neighbors so you can mirror Jesus' love to them in a more authentic way.

As you stop to reflect on how much information you were able to complete, let me say again—please, sweet sister, don't let this create unnecessary guilt. Grace on, guilt off. Remember, when the Lord brings conviction, He does it to lead us to freedom, not to pile on shame. This exercise should be used as a bridge to reconcile the reality of how well we know our neighbors with the goal of Jesus' Great Commandment.

I think we can all handle that. And want that.

I grew up in the church where I colored hundreds of "love your neighbor" Sunday school sheets. Yet as many ways as I've played around the edges of this foundational teaching of Scripture throughout my life, I've decided now to rip down all those pictures in my mind and tear them up. No more coloring. No more pretending. I'm determined to put love into action.

I'm on my knees at this moment—with my grid laid out in front of me—convicted to fill in many more lines this year. And I'm begging the One who modeled love unconditionally, "Lord Jesus, please show me how to love my neighbors as myself."

Won't you join me?

Dear Jen

I admit, I don't know my neighbors, but I already get together with friends from work and church, so this feels like one more thing on my to-do list.

Do I Have To?

Dear Do I Have To,

Remember, grace on, guilt off. There are no have-tos here except loving God and loving others, and yet there are many benefits from being in community with your neighbors. Even though I love living out in the country, I often wish I was in a closer neighborhood, where you don't have to drive anywhere to begin investing in the lives of those who live right next door, and it offers so many benefits. Like:

1. *Camaraderie.* Everything is better when you do life together. Why not attempt to build camaraderie where it can happen naturally, like outside your front door? It's a wonderful place to learn more about diverse backgrounds, experiences, and lifestyles.

2. *Pooled fun.* For National Night Out (first Tuesday of August), organize your first block party, rent inflatable water slides, and cool off together. Fourth of July bash? Share the expense of fireworks and food. Initiate Friday Fun Nights. My friend Shellie's neighborhood purchased an outdoor inflatable movie screen. They planned a Star Wars Summer Bonanza, and each home took turns hosting a movie night in the back-yard. The kids dressed up as their favorite characters, no one had to clean their house, and summer memories were made.

Or plan a neighborhood yard sale together. You'd be amazed at the bonding that occurs as you sell off treasures and reminisce about their history. One young mom, pregnant and in need of mentoring and friendship, hosted a yard sale I attended. I left her driveway with a phone number, and our relationship has stretched nearly twenty years. All from a neighborhood yard sale.

3. *Helping one another out.* The more you develop relationships with your neighbors, the more you'll notice a "got your back" spirit of cooperation developing. Many hands make light work.

Offer to ease a neighbor's load with yard work after a sickness. Help move fallen trees after thunderstorms or shovel out of snowstorms together, then warm up with hot chocolate. Offer to pick up UPS packages if a neighbor leaves on vacation. Stuff like that.

Having a built-in support system is another step toward living out the Great Commandment. Make sure your neighbors have your cell phone number in case of an emergency, and assure them you're the one to call at 2:00 in the morning if necessary.

And yes, you really can borrow a cup of sugar from your neighbor rather than driving to the store.

Investing in your neighbors offers all these benefits and more, plus it breaks down walls of division that may have been unintentionally erected.

Jen

Elevate the Ordinary

❀ Are you ready to elevate your neighborhood relationships? My friend shared how a new couple moved onto their street and declared, "We want to get to know everyone. Let's make a difference in this neighborhood." They swooped in, became the neighborhood ambassadors, and changed the entire culture of how people neighbored. In a few short years it's become a close-knit community. Are you up for that same challenge? Pick one activity to begin connecting with those who live closest to you. Here are a few ideas I've seen done with great success.

❀ Any reason to gather for food: neighborhood potluck, Cinco de Mayo, Super Bowl, or World Series parties. Progressive dinners, a Friday night food truck tradition, or a street cookout for local law enforcement to thank them for their service.

❀ Parades planned and executed by the kids, Christmas caroling, s'mores, and bonfires.

❀ Send a "Welcome to the Neighborhood" printable with recommended doctors, dentists, restaurants, family fun activities, churches, and personalized suggestions.

❀ Backyard movie nights, "Bring a Yard Game" night, Ladies Night Out, neighborhood bunco.

❀ Add a free library for book sharing.

❀ Create a private neighborhood Facebook group or send a weekly e-mail newsletter. Include a photo directory with names, addresses, interests, and birthdays. Allow information for upcoming events, community issues, classified ads, help with lawn care, lost pets, etc. After events happen, encourage people to post pictures to create excitement for future participation.

7

The Power of One

~~∽∾⟳⟳∾~~

$\mathcal{J}$ sat in my college classroom as my religion professor executed a math problem that both stunned me and revolutionized how I invested my time in ministry. As we discussed the benefits of mentoring, he demonstrated the multiplication process that occurs if each one of us would purposefully invest in the life of one other person for a year.

I've never been much of a math girl, but even I could clearly see the exponential power of what he was describing. If each of us came alongside just one person each year—doing life with them, discipling and teaching them about the Bible, unpacking how it interacts and impacts all aspects of their life—and then encouraged them to do the same thing with another person the next year, do you know what would happen? In the course of our one lifetime, *hundreds of thousands* would be touched by what we started.

See, I wasn't exaggerating when I said, "One invitation really can change a generation."

As I think back on key milestones in my own life, every single one is marked by an investment from one woman committed to sharing life with me for a season. Their impact wasn't the result of a larger-than-life platform or words crafted for their blog. No, my life was changed through seemingly everyday encounters with women who believed in the beauty of being deeply rooted right where God had placed them. They weren't looking to be launched into a bigger opportunity. They knew (and know) that God had entrusted them to be present and faithful in their immediate sphere of influence.

Debbie. Her wisdom poured out as she invited me to meet weekly and study the classic Richard Foster book *Celebration of Discipline.* Her desire to raise up the next generation of leaders moved me. She didn't dumb down our topics but believed a sixteen-year-old girl could change the world given the right foundation. Now I believe the same thing for my own daughters.

Jan. Her kitchen prowess taught me to cook and use the gifts of treats as a vehicle to minister to the needs of so much more than a hungry tummy. Now I've witnessed how a cold cup of water and a hot meal can woo the soul.

Faye. She demonstrated the importance of shoring up my communication skills so I could boldly proclaim and defend my worldview. Now I live in a culture where truth is considered relative, yet I know the source of absolute truth.

Rachel. She lives with intention and purpose. My sister-in-law's been my sounding board as we've challenged each other deeply in our mothering, our marriages, and our faith. We ask the hard questions and aren't afraid of the answers. Now we encourage others to embrace life with abandon.

But it was, and still is, my mom—above all—whose love, faithfulness, and consistency influence me more than any other. The reason I know Jesus is because my mom modeled His love and because I wanted what she had. I open my home today because she opened her home. I prioritize family because she did it so well.

That's the power of one touching another.

In fact, it almost can't be helped when we do.

A while back I received an e-mail from a girl who, more than fifteen years ago, had lived with us for six weeks. I've lost touch with most of those we've hosted, so I never know the rest of their stories, but she came across my blog one day and wrote to share with me a bit of her heart.

Maybe this is one of those things where you left a mark on my life and you don't even remember me. Or even like me. But I remember you, and I remember the night I said you looked like your dad and you told me you were adopted.

I never forgot a lot of things. Like seeing a real Christian family live their life. Homeschooling. Loving discipline. Intentionally leaving a heritage of Christ. Bearing up under tough times.

After adopting our oldest daughter, I still thought about you. And I just wanted you to know I never forgot, and it impacts me now as a wife and mother.

Her words left me stunned. Here's why.

The time when we opened our guest room to her, our four children were sharing a room, and I was struggling to do anything well. I liked her, but I didn't feel warm and welcoming toward her during those weeks. (Honestly, I probably wasn't, since she questioned if I even remembered her . . . or *liked* her.) I didn't prioritize time to invest in her as a young woman—not because I didn't want to, but because I was overwhelmed with wrangling our kiddos and keeping the house clean and getting our meals ready, and I certainly didn't think she was paying attention.

But I learned a lot about following Jesus after reading Jessica's e-mail. Because even though all I remember from those six weeks is being one hot mess, He still chose me to champion His love. I didn't have to get my act together before He could use me. I was just a willing and available mess who desired to be used for His glory.

The power of one never grows old—the beauty that stems from life-on-life, one-on-one relationships. And you know what? You get to be part of that life-giving multiplication process. You are the someone God wants to use now to impact this next generation. Your unique gift, your untold story, your broken and mended heart, your fierce love, your brave authenticity—all these intricate threads woven together create a tapestry He wants to use to unveil His love to someone who needs to experience it. You are the one who can meet the need of another today if you just open the door.

Or maybe even a sofa.

We have an old, down-filled sofa that gets a lot of use. So many people have slept there that now its feathers are poking into people's behinds whenever they sit or lie down. But I hate to see it go because it holds so many meaningful memories. Memories of late-night discussions about

God. Memories covering the pros and cons of dating. Memories uncovering struggles with peer pressure. Memories of changed lives.

Like Antoine.

"Some of you know my story," he started in, standing humbly before my extended family during one of our traditional times of deep sharing. "There's a lot to tell about my background. It was pretty dysfunctional. The Schmidts were the first gospel-centered family I'd ever encountered. I didn't know what it looked like before. But now they've welcomed me into their family. And not only do I feel like they've adopted me, but I've been adopted into the family of God. There's no place better to be."

Those words wrecked me. I glanced out of the corner of my eyes to confirm the tears I knew were streaming down my husband's face as well. We hadn't done much at all. We'd simply opened our door, scrounged up some meals, and offered him our sofa.

Our family friendship with Antoine started in such a small way. One afternoon after football practice, our teen boys barged through the door. I could smell them before I heard them. Think of the wretched gag reflex that assails you when you finally root out that rotten potato, the one that's gotten buried in the bottom of your pantry. Got it? Only imagine something *worse* than that, times two, and you're close to what I was smelling. Standing in the laundry room, dripping with so much sweat I could wring out a gallon full if they'd let me, they announced their new football friend was here for dinner.

But without warning, one friend became two, which doubled to four, by which the multiplication process snowballed, until I was praying a full-on, food-stretching miracle over my "five loaves and two fish," knowing they would need to feed eight—*eight!*—high school football players, in addition to my own.

Ranging in age from seventeen to nineteen, these boy-men attended a local boarding school where our sons joined them on the same football team. And pretty soon, at least two to three nights a week, our packed table represented five different states, with varying social, racial, and economic backgrounds.

For many of them, their common denominator was what they were lacking (strong families) as well as what they were gaining (hope for the future through football). And when the weekend rolled around, they all shared a common fatigue for the school's strict curfew policy and cafeteria meals, so they'd sign out and sleep at our house. Bodies stretched everywhere—each couch filled, double bunk beds on overload, even air mattresses tucked into corners. And the bodily noises coming from those areas? I'll leave it at that.

Those days were loud, tiring, and unpredictable. In the guys' minds I was their short-order cook. (Although, isn't that the life of all parents?) "What's your mom making?" was what I heard regularly echoing down the hall, as God reminded me daily to keep on keeping on. *It's only for a season, a super-short season.* Each evening I'd fall into bed completely spent, having learned that flexibility is required for much more than gymnastics. When some of my friends would say, "Jen, that stresses me out just thinking about it," I'd remind myself this was a choice. *Do I desire to maintain our status quo, or do I desire to make a difference?*

To tell you the truth, sometimes I didn't know the answer to that question. Because I wanted my comfort back. I like my Netflix, my coffee, and my quiet time. And this deluge of hungry boys in my house was ruffling my feathers a bit. Sometimes I was ready to shut both the door and the fridge.

First Peter 4:8–9 (NIV) came to mind: "Above all, love each other deeply. . . . Offer hospitality to one another without grumbling," without complaining. My attitude reminded me of when our kids were younger and I'd ask them to do something. While often obedient, they'd trudge through the motions. I'd always remind them, "Do it with a happy heart, please." I could almost hear Peter reminding me of the same thing because there was definitely some grumbling under my breath.

But that was only on the days when I forgot my original desire: to glorify God and make Him known. This wasn't about me. Life-giving hospitality is never about us. It's a journey to surrender control, to present our seemingly insignificant offering to Him. It's about stewarding the one thing before us well, becoming an unlikely messenger for the gospel, and pointing it all back to Him.

The power of one.

The Lord did a major work in all of us during those months. We laughed hard . . . really hard. We lingered and listened to lots of stories around the table. And we all learned a lot of things together. We heard firsthand how a few of these babies had been forced to grow up overnight, fending for themselves at an early age. This was the first time in our sons' lives that they'd been in the minority, and they learned to listen with more than their ears, to understand the heart story of their friends.

Before long, though, the guys started scooting out and heading back to school on Saturday afternoon, after we'd put a boundary in place, declaring that whoever spends the night on Saturday wakes up and goes to church with us on Sunday. Like family. Only one guy was left standing after that.

And that guy was Antoine.

The hopeful tears I cry now are for the beautiful way God has been and is working mightily in Antoine's life. He was here again this past weekend. When you're young and single and sleep is overrated, you don't think twice about a spontaneous seven-hour drive. And he knows he's always welcome. He's family.

Gathered around the same table that hosted him all those years ago, we reminisced about that season. We listened to him telling us about nuggets of wisdom learned from the new books he'd devoured and heard about the ways additional men have come alongside him in discipleship roles. Many times I've regretted that I didn't do enough to penetrate the hearts of all eight of those boys. (My husband wisely reminds me that we have no clue what God is doing with those other seeds we planted.)

But here's one. Antoine. A whole new legacy began for him when he named Jesus as Lord. A clean slate, his do-over. By surrendering our sofa and a spot in the boys' room, God did something that changed a generation. He slays me with the knowledge of that.

To witness the power of one in action is both humbling and overwhelming.

As Antoine was packing up to leave, I scrounged around trying to find him some snacks. "I need to send you on the road with food. Here, I have some Krispy Kreme doughnuts."

"Sounds good, but don't worry, I always take one of these meal replacement shakes, so I'm fine."

"Do you know what's in those things?" (Says the one trying to shove doughnuts on him.) "They can't replace the value of whole foods. I need to send you with some fruit. How about a bag of carrots? I have an apple, a pear, and a clementine. They're easy to peel."

"I'll take the apple."

"Are you sure? That's all? I want to fill you up, and that's not enough for the road."

"It doesn't matter what food you feed me. I always leave here filled." (Gulp.)

Becoming women of significance doesn't start with a microphone or a stage or even a blog following. It doesn't depend on special talents or a larger-than-life personality. It begins by simply saying, "Yes, Lord, I'm willing to be just one simple person. Here's my one door, my one table, my one sofa. Use them."

That's because simple everyday steps of faithfulness *are* our platform. Somehow in the middle of our unqualified mess, we become women of influence. There's power in just starting with one.

Just open up your one door. Willingly share your one table. Offer up your one secondhand sofa. Then watch God use these small offerings to change one life forever . . . and who knows how many hundreds or thousands more as He multiplies.

Dear Jen

I've been following your Instagram feed that's filled with photos of teens in your home all the time. As your kids have gotten older, how have you handled kids that are a bad influence? I'm conflicted and need direction. My teen daughter, since making a new friend, has become moody, vulgar, and disrespectful.

I know no one is perfect, least of all me, but this scares me, and I really messed up with how I handled it. Should I allow them to continue spending time together?

Conflicted

Dear Conflicted,

This is a challenging question with no easy answer. We've definitely been through these situations, and we pleaded for the Lord's guidance and wisdom. I can't speak to your exact situation, but I do know these two truths: it is not your young daughter's responsibility to bring this girl to the Lord, and it is your job to protect and nurture your daughter.

You can still practice hospitality by inviting the teen girl over for dinner, loving on her, and having her spend quality time with your family, but I recommend that you keep their interaction limited to supervised situations without sleepovers for a time. As moms, we need to run interference in situations like these.

If you've handled this situation poorly with your daughter, as you say, go humbly and ask for forgiveness. As parents we aren't always going to get it right, and we will make mistakes on the way. Confess this to her. Tell her how much you love her, but also tell her it's your job to guide and protect her at this tender age and that you are doing what you feel is best right now. Let her know, too, that this decision may change as you monitor things, and then pray, pray, pray.

Jen

Elevate the Ordinary

❁ As your home becomes a place where kids like to hang out, boundaries are healthy. A lot of freedom comes within those boundaries.

❁ Create a shelf in your pantry that is open for business. Stock it with fun snacks and drinks that kids love, and let them know they can help themselves to those specific foods, but anything else is off limits. Freedom, yet boundaries.

❁ Once kids have spent more than three full days at our house, I treat them like family. We have such fun together, but if my kids have chores, I don't let them off the hook just because their friend is over. (We'd never get anything done.) Their friends can join right in. After that initiation, I engage with their friends like I do my own kids. This creates a level of authenticity, and it invites accountability as they deepen relationships. I know I've reached the "friend goals" we've established in our home when my kids' friends start calling me "Momma Jen" or "Momma Schmidt." This year, I even got a few Mother's Day texts from them. Day made.

One Family, One Gospel

When you enter the Schmidt family home, you'll always find laughter, a little clutter here and there, and a welcoming of guests at any time. It doesn't take long to feel a part of the family and become enamored by their love for one another.

In August 2010, I met them while attending classes and playing football with their two oldest sons. From the first time I met Jen and Gregg, their smiles were infectious. I never would have imagined the significance of this divine appointment. Every weekend or so, I would spend fall nights there watching football, playing video games and outdoor sports, and going on adventures with the boys, under one condition: I had to attend church on Sunday. I had no reservations about attending church. In fact, it made me feel like one of their children. I cannot recall one instance where I was told it would not be a good weekend to visit.

Prior to meeting the Schmidt family, I had never been around a gospel-driven family. I didn't have a saving faith despite going to church once in a while as a kid. The weekends at the Schmidts became formative for who I was to become. I became immersed in a gospel rhythm unbeknown to me. They showed me what life looked like, not in Adam but in Christ. I will never be able to repay them for their hospitality.

One of the things that seemed to bind them together was food. Whether it was Wendy's, frozen pizza, or one of Jen's experimental dishes, their family always seemed to eat together. When I was growing up, my mom worked relentlessly, and I didn't live with my dad, so meals in my home were often nothing more than a means of nourishment. I can recall countless times when I ate dinner in my bedroom alone. The Schmidts displayed something brand-new to me: using mealtime to unify their family. At the time I wasn't aware the gospel was the driving force behind their lives.

They also demonstrated many things about everyday life that were new and eye-opening to me. I had never before talked about finances, so some of their spending habits appeared absurd. For example, one time their son Taylor fed all his friends fast food by charging his parents' credit card without their permission. A few days later, once his parents checked their credit card activity, he was reprimanded severely. I failed to comprehend what was wrong with his using it. I didn't understand the value of a dollar, so discussions on the right ways to use and steward money were new to me. Also, many weekends, the Schmidts would pop in frozen pizzas for us guys. I can probably count on one hand the number of times I'd eaten frozen pizza before because it's always better to have pizza delivered from a local pizzeria. I was shocked when they said they'd never had pizza delivered before because it's so much more expensive. It's funny the things you notice when you live with someone.

As I grow as a man, I become more appreciative of the exposure the Schmidt family has provided me, not only to things like budgeting and stewardship but to all of life and especially the gospel.

8

Food for Thought

I tore through the front door looking for my sister-in-law, otherwise known as my sister-in-love, otherwise known as my best friend since high school, otherwise known as the girl who became a prospective date for my brother only after I insisted he ask her out or he'd forever reap the wrath from refusing his little sister's advice.

"Rach? Rach? Where are you?" I rushed in, flung my arms around her, and announced with no less flare than Scarlet O'Hara, "I think I've met the guy I'm going to marry! If it's not him, it's going to be someone just like him."

I plopped down on her sofa, slightly out of breath from the excitement, and continued with what I'd hurried over so fast to tell her.

"I know it sounds crazy, Rach, but you know I've never said anything like this before." (Factually, I didn't date much through college, so that was a moot point.)

"He loves Jesus. He's a great conversationalist. He was in FCA. He's hot. He's funny." (Come to find out, he was reciting old movie lines, but by the time I found out they weren't originals, I was already hooked.)

"Let me back up and tell you all about it." (I could barely get the words out fast enough. Life as I knew it had changed in twenty-four hours.)

But here's the really sounds-crazy part. Because believe it or not, this all came about from a God-instilled passion in me for gathering people and feeding them well. And, no, I'm not kidding.

Now let me back up and tell YOU all about THAT.

Someone once told me, "Jen, you're a gatherer of people." *A gatherer of people.* I like that. It's a label I can embrace now, but I must confess that it came from intimately understanding the feeling of being alone, of missing out, of not feeling like part of the crowd. It came from being picked last for games. It came from being the girl in college who was deemed every guy's best friend but never the one chosen to date. Even now it comes from seeing friends posting pictures of their most recent get-togethers and wondering why I wasn't invited. Sometimes those feelings aren't easy to shake. But because of all those old wounds, God has given me a deep desire to prevent anyone else from feeling that way. More importantly, I want to point others to the only One who can truly fill those lonely spots. I've developed this shepherding mentality— introducing strangers, making room for one more, and never wanting someone sitting alone if it can be helped.

During college I first realized that one of the easiest ways to build a bridge to friendships was through food and gathering around the table. This proved to be the quickest way to create meaningful companionship and connection. While food is obviously a means for satisfying hunger, it can also provide the occasion for table fellowship, which holds the power to revolutionize the way families and friends connect. Everything's deeper at the table. Community's sweeter, laughter's louder, stories richer, heartache heavier.

Oops, got stuck in a bit of a tangent there. But you can see how seriously, how passionately I feel about this.

Back now to my Scarlett-like declaration.

New Year's Eve was fast approaching, and my best girlfriends and I needed a plan. They were pushing me to host a party at my apartment, but fitting ten friends in such a cramped space all night would need some ninja-like brainstorming.

We opted instead for the best of both worlds—a New Year's Day brunch. As single girls with so many plans and too little time, this solution allowed us to enjoy visiting a few other parties the night before and then relax the next day during a casual mid-morning gathering with our closest friends.

Plus, brunches are my jam. In fact, anything breakfast is my jam. Friends love when I serve breakfast for dinner. It invites a more casual atmosphere. Breakfast recipes are easy to make ahead of time, they're fairly inexpensive, and even the pickiest of eaters can find something they like.

So I was pumped about our New Year's brunch. And since everyone coming was a dear friend, I decided a low-maintenance morning was in order. I can't underscore enough how casual I kept it. I rolled out of bed and put my hair in a Pebbles Flintstone ponytail—literally a ponytail sprout sticking straight out of the top of my head. (Don't ask me what I was thinking. I wasn't.) And to top it off, I stayed in my purple-checked, flannel PJs (Wisconsin winters are brutal) and applied no makeup except mascara because for natural blonds it's nearly impossible to get away without a little help on our lashes.

Right at the beginning of brunch, right as the food was starting to make its way to the table, a ministry friend who lived a few blocks away called and asked if his accountant roommate could come eat with us before he made his way to work. Yes, I know it was a holiday, but he detailed a long sob story about how his friend, despite already putting in long hours on New Year's Eve, was heading into the office again on New Year's Day. My friend was convinced that this brunch was the solution to getting his roommate out of the house. Not one to turn away a stray in need of a little nourishment, I replied, "Of course, bring him over. I'll feed him."

Ten minutes later, that poor, nerdy guy walked up my stairs . . . looking like no accountant I'd ever met.

I wondered if he could hear how hard my heart was beating as I greeted him. I got him something to drink, and then ever so discreetly, I excused myself to my bedroom. Oh, yes, I did. Ripping out that Pebbles ponytail, I fluffed my hair and put on a little makeup, going from low maintenance to at least mid maintenance. Unfortunately, changing into some cute jeans would have been too obvious, so it was flannel pajamas for the win.

As we passed the plate of hash-brown casserole, we all shared bits of ourselves. And by the time the French toast bake had circled again, we'd all told our faith story. As we topped off our time together over dessert, this guy had ticked the box on all the qualities I'd mentally pinpointed for a future husband. I kept thinking, "It's too good to be true." Five hours later, with a full tummy, that nerdy accountant closed down my party. He never did go to work.

My sister-in-law, hanging on every detail, squealed. "I cannot believe that all happened today and I missed it. What's this guy's name?"

"Dave. His name is Dave," I blurted out immediately.

Uh, Gregg, actually. (Close.) But fourteen months later, I was married to Gregg the accountant. We still chuckle about the fact that it took me a few weeks to figure out the correct first name of my dream man. But no worries: in honor of my faux pas, we named our third son (you guessed it) David.

Can you even believe how all of that came about? If I hadn't already been a firm believer in the radical power behind imperfect hospitality, that New Year's brunch would have changed my mind all by itself. No one wants to sound like a matchmaking grandma who reminds us that the way to a man's heart is through his stomach. And I certainly don't tell single girls that gathering around a table will snag them a hubby. But in this case, it worked for me.

I often wonder what would have happened if I hadn't opened the door.

What if I'd decided that I was too tired from our New Year's Eve festivities to welcome people into my apartment? What if I didn't understand God's delight when we celebrate together through a shared meal? So many things could have prevented this life-changing meeting from happening. My husband and I have pondered this. Based on our busy schedules, and the fact that he had made both a personal resolution, as well as a public announcement, that he was not going to date until he was done with his master's program, it would have been years before we met, if at all.

But two years after we met, as he was finally finishing that master's program, he studied for his finals while bouncing a honeymoon baby on his leg. God has a sense of humor. Never say never.

I'm forever grateful that this simple act of eating together represented something so much bigger. I'm grateful it meant friendship and belonging and a roommate who cared enough to extend an invite. Or else I'd be writing a whole different story.

What else have we failed to see about the importance of gathering around the table?

Long before the Internet or Facebook, the table was the first and most important social platform ever built. Gathering around the table has been at the epicenter of relationships long before any of us hosted our first meal. A meeting place for connection and community, food and table time have always been distinct markers in kingdom building.

Yet recently a shift's occurred. I'm sure you've noticed it.

When we add up the amount of time afforded us to dine together throughout our lives, the resulting sum comes as a shock. By the time we reach our fortieth birthday, we will have eaten forty thousand meals and spent more than forty thousand hours in a food-related atmosphere. Yet right now, we as a society eat one out of every five meals in our cars, and more than half of American children eat a fast-food meal every single day. We now recognize the drive-through restaurant workers better than our neighbors, and we can't remember the last time we've actually lingered over a meal.

Please hear me: I do understand a bit of this double-edged tension. We have to eat to live, yet our schedules resemble a thousand-piece puzzle, and therefore something has to give. That's what makes the lure of the drive-through so real. I get it. While I've reiterated gathering at the table as one of the focal points of family life, I have no room for guilt shaming here because the drive-through has saved me more than once. But still . . . *every day?*

I just don't want us to miss out on what could have been. I don't want us to pile up the regrets of afterthoughts because we didn't fight with all our might for something so simple—so basic—that could have changed the course of a generation.

Whenever we drop the habit of spending mealtimes together and we have no sense of urgency to prioritize it, we lose an open invitation to the most important moment of the day—a forum for opinion and nuances; a sounding board that combats a crisis of culture; inexpensive therapy with a side of unstructured, open communication. It's a time for sharing problems but rarely with the forced offering of "this is the way" type of solutions. People pay a lot of money for times like these, and it's ours for free. Every day. If we'll take it.

How can we afford to deprioritize this time-honored tradition that holds the utmost importance from days of old, one that's based around a fundamental pattern we see outlined in Scripture? Why do we consistently overlook one of the simplest pleasures—to linger, savor, and enjoy our time at the table? The practices of breaking bread together and setting apart time for the table are an art we must model if we want it passed down from generation to generation. If we ever allow ourselves to forget the importance attached to these simple yet sacred moments, our knowledge of the art itself begins to fade slowly.

For me, the kitchen is the heartbeat of our home. It's where the senses are engaged, a place where people are drawn to linger. The aroma of baked goods, the flickering candlelight during the evening meal (even when it's frozen pizza and boxed macaroni), the cut flowers donning the Mason jars (dandelion weeds picked by our daughter), and the soft music floating in the background are only a precursor to the cornerstone of life found around the table. There's really nothing like it.

Yesterday, for example, our daughters made chocolate chip cookies while I finished up on a work deadline. Our son rushed home from school to find such nostalgic smells permeating the kitchen, and the first words out of his mouth—"Mom, I smell my favorite cookies"—affirmed just how quickly we tie senses together in creating special memories through food. Even the slow-cooking scent of frozen chicken and barbecue sauce I'd dumped in the Crock-Pot elicited a response, causing him to wonder aloud when we were sitting down for dinner.

This is what I want for our children. We're cultivating a lifestyle of table fellowship so that they'll be able to think back, not just on the meals eaten here, but on the life we've wrestled through and the stories lived out around our table. I want the table to be a place that reflects sacred moments and a love of nurturing life. Because when the mundane and the magnificent intersect around the table, a sense of identity is forged. The table allows for those holy moments to happen when we slow down and let them. Meals together serve as small acts with significant importance. It's where we and they shape our worldview, process our history, dissect our theology, debate our politics, and both confront and restore relationships. All are allowed to flourish at our table.

Yet never assume the table comes with set rules or best practices. There is no "one right way" to gather, to feed, to welcome. While I've savored five-course, formal meals around a European table, mesmerized by the ambiance, one of my most intimate dining experiences occurred in a dilapidated, Third-World, open-air hut. Nestled around a wobbling wooden box with my legs and feet coated in a layer of grime from the dirt floor, a new sister and I sipped "coffee," although I'm pretty certain it was brown water. The home's stove—a crackling fire—provided an environment which far surpassed fine dining. And though the bread we broke had the consistency of cement, unbridled emotion poured from my precious host. Tears streamed down her cheeks as she laid her heart bare, broken by some devastating choices her daughter had made. I wrapped my arms around her, and we wept together. I cried for her daughter. I cried for my own of the same age. And right then, amid the free-range chickens pecking at our feet, our differences dissipated. Our commonalities bound us: two helpless mommas seeking and storming the gates of heaven for the hearts of our children. That's the power of the table, the great equalizer. Two sisters are better than one.

God's voice got my attention—starting as a whisper yet becoming nearly audible by the end of our makeshift meal: *Do you see Me? Do you hear Me? Jen, do you taste Me in the midst of this moment? It's a bit of My kingdom brought to earth, isn't it?*

Yes, I heard Him loud and clear. I wasn't sure what He was asking of me. But I knew this table represented something of significant importance for my hungry heart. I took a deep breath, reveling in the holiness of the moment. Convicted and disarmed, I came away from that table time with a renewed sense of fervor for this radical mission of hospitality. How can we not fight for these pivotal moments?

Yes, fight. For a seat around the table. For everybody.

A few years ago, I served as a spokeswoman for a major food brand to encourage bringing family and friends back to the table. As a result of substantial research, my own thoughts began orbiting around a central theme that merged: mealtime is the primary avenue to connectedness.

As a result, I started a food blog offering simple, homemade recipe options—"10 Minute Dinners." The blog's tagline was, "Less time around the stove, more time around the table," because I realized our society is hungry to gather but often feels overwhelmed with knowing where to begin.

The majority of U.S. families admit to eating only one meal together out of five days during the week, and even that one meal is often in front of the television. Sixty years ago, families and friends spent an average of *ninety minutes* around the table, whereas today it consists of less than twelve minutes. If any. Our fast-paced living doesn't allow for more. Is it any wonder then that the average parent spends only 38.5 minutes *per week* in meaningful conversation with their children?[8] Or that nearly half of all adults eat the majority of their meals alone?[9]

As we lose the table, we lose a generation of lives intertwined for His glory. God has always known the substance that food brings to both our bodies and our souls. And the more I began to understand the scope of how often the act of eating together is mentioned in both the Old and New Testaments, the more I'm convinced that food is one of the building blocks of our faith. In fact, the more I dive specifically into the meals of Jesus, the more fervent I become about including simple offerings of food and drink in our practice of hospitality.

I've been spending time in the book of Luke lately, and I think he'd be the first Bible personality I'd invite to my table. More than any of the other Gospel writers, Luke seemed to understand the significance of mealtime. I imagine him as the quintessential New Testament food blogger, whipping out his cell phone to capture in pictures what can't be described with words. He'd bring to life the significance of food and community. After all, food was mentioned around fifty times in his Gospel. Robert Karris observes, "In Luke's Gospel, Jesus is either going to a meal, at a meal, or coming from a meal."[10]

Jesus used the sharing of food throughout His ministry as an opportunity for nourishment on so many levels: to break down barriers, bring community together, radically cross economic boundaries, and even give opposing enemies the opportunity to sit together. Essentially, "Jesus ate good food with bad people."[11] He understood the role food plays in ministry. The context behind many of Jesus' interactions with His followers was a simple meal. He modeled its importance, and yet Luke seems to be the only one who highlighted this in his writing. Maybe he didn't want us to miss out on Jesus' simple yet revolutionary method.

We can learn and apply a lot from this. In *A Meal with Jesus,* author Tim Chester poses an interesting question in the introduction: "How would you complete this sentence—The Son of Man came . . ."[12] Out of curiosity, I used my husband and son as my testing group, and they followed suit with the majority of Christians. They answered, "The Son of Man came not to be served but to serve, and to give his life as a ransom for many" (Mark 10:45 ESV), followed by, "The Son of Man came to seek and to save the lost" (Luke 19:10 ESV).

So then I probed. "There's a third way to respond." They were as stumped as I had been previously. The third response is, "The Son of Man has come eating and drinking" (Luke 7:34 ESV).

My husband argued, "Oh, no, He didn't."

"Oh, yes, He did. Open the Bible and I'll show you." How is it that I'd glossed over that last statement when I'd read it so often? Chester writes, "The first two are statements of purpose. *Why* did Jesus come? He came to serve, to give his life as a ransom, to seek and save the lost. The third statement is a statement of method."[13] It's *how* Jesus came— eating and drinking. Isn't that a dynamic insight? How brilliant that His gospel strategy was often disguised as a long, lingering meal stretching out past sunset. He didn't spend time creating more corporate planning strategy meetings or growing new church programs. *He simply fed more.* He intertwined His message and His method in such an authentic and natural way that we almost miss it.

Jesus came "eating and drinking," and it blew people's minds. That's because when He sat down to eat, there was a lot more going on than just the savoring of fresh fish hot off the grill, a loaf of bread, and a cool drink. Doing life around the table was (and is) one of His favorite ways to enact world change—one of His most profound yet simple strategies for discipleship, evangelism, and the encouragement of the saints. So let's take His lead. Set the table. Set your heart. Then with great anticipation, set your eyes on the One who gathers us at the table in the first place.

Dear Jen

As I read this, I feel so guilty. I know how important it is to eat as a family, but I'm so exhausted after working full-time. By the time I pick up the kids from day care, it's much easier to grab food to go. Then you mention eating by candlelight and inviting someone else to the table, and I want to throw in the towel.

Mom Guilt

Dear Mom Guilt,

First of all, big hugs here from a Chick-fil-A junkie. I've done my share of drive-through visits. Some seasons of life make spending concentrated time at the table more difficult than others.

The years with small children are particularly exhausting, so start with little things. Casting a long-term legacy begins with one small step toward intentionality and then guarding the importance of that single step. Look at your schedule and begin by setting a reasonable goal.

- Find pockets of time that make eating together four times a week possible.
- Enjoy meals together other than dinner. Saturday morning pancakes are always a fun, food tradition. When our busy sports schedules collided, dinners with all seven of us were nearly impossible, but we committed to being home in time for dessert.
- Make it fun. Sometimes we ate dinner *under* the table, or we started with dessert first, while I warned them to "save room for those yummy peas."
- Keep your together-time technology-free. No phones or TV. That means us, too, mommas. Gather the phones and put them away. Remember, it's not about a rule of law but about the spirit of gathering. Just make sure that once you set aside those times of eating together, you guard them like it's your job.

Oh, and about those candles? Believe it or not, lighting candles at the table is a tradition that began when our kids were tiny. Lighting the candles and turning on soft music gave me a brief moment to settle my soul and pretend the house wasn't in shambles. For as long as it took them to eat, I had things under control. Everything is better by candlelight. Try it. Even when we had frozen pizza or I brought home fast food, we'd eat it at the table by candlelight. It's a tradition we still continue.

Jen

Elevate the Ordinary

❀ Have fun with your table setting tonight. No need for fancy dishes. I never registered for china, and twenty-four years later I still don't regret that decision. I invested in twelve place settings of a simple white, filigree pattern that I can mix and match with anything. We still use them today.

❀ White dishes are fun to accessorize and never go out of style. Use colorful bowls or plates and napkins to layer and add a pop of color. A creative napkin fold can really bring a place setting to life. For festive occasions, I've paired white dishes with gold charger plates and fresh cut greenery from our yard. When long tables have needed something special, I've created beautiful table runners out of unique wrapping paper cut to size, and no one was the wiser. Check the dollar stores for a surprisingly great selection of dishes and glassware.

❀ Bring a little extra beauty tonight. Take a few additional minutes and set the table with something out of the ordinary that keeps the family wondering, "What's the special occasion?"

9

The Potluck:
Risks and Rewards

*A*n open home, like an open table, is the overflow of an open heart. And the best, most open table of them all is the potluck—whether it features the warm, hearty tastes of the Midwest where I was born and raised, or the home-style flavors of the South where I enjoy them now with North Carolina barbecue, slaw, and banana pudding. Or anywhere in between.

My heart sure does love a potluck.

All my childhood potluck memories swirl amid my aunts' kitchens. My dad's side of the family would gather at one of their homes for all the traditional holidays, with a few birthdays mixed in, and I anticipated those rare times together throughout the year with hungry expectation.

As soon as I'd arrive, I'd search out my grandpa first. He never failed to remind this baby of the bunch that she was his favorite. I'm pretty certain he said the same thing to each of the grandkids—all the other cousins who were swarming throughout the house. But it didn't matter; we all knew we were each the favorite, no matter what the rest of them thought. On command he'd snort a new nickel from his nose or do a little sleight of hand where he'd miraculously seem to yank the tip of his thumb right off at the knuckle. But while the wonder of his "magic" tricks wore off after a few years, our love and affection for Grandpa only grew.

After the initial greetings, younger cousins would be ushered down to the basement to find the nearest board game. Others would scramble for the best recliner positions with high hopes of a victorious Packers game. My aunts? They donned their aprons and worked for hours while the familiar smells of their tried-and-true recipes slowly reached every corner of the house. I'd race into the kitchen to check on progress, peek at the table to see it piled high with the fruits of their labor, and then open the oven, hoping there'd be enough strawberry-rhubarb pie to go around.

Thirty years later I still remember late-night evenings of storytelling, my grandpa reminding us, "You ain't much if you ain't Dutch," and the men recounting their white-water fishing adventures in Canada. Each year the tales grew larger, but so did the laughter. Being the baby girl, well removed in age from those expeditions, I sat up and listened a little harder in hopes that someday, just maybe, I could go along on the same type of adventure.

On many visits, I fell sound asleep on my aunt's couch to the sound of the ladies gathered in the kitchen, the men shooed out to the back porch so my grandpa could smoke his pipe. Sometime during the late hours, my dad would load me into the station wagon with the seats laid down (no belt laws in the good ol' days), and as he carried me to bed, he'd pop a kiss on my forehead with the reassurance, "Shhh, shhh, go back to sleep." I always did. Immediately.

Ahh, good days. Good days.

Family gatherings on my mom's side, however, don't hold the same fond memories as those joyful potlucks. When you're stepping into a generational legacy steeped in deep scars from years of abuse, you tiptoe around every conversation wondering what might ignite a carefully hidden land mine. Alcoholism turns the potential for meaningful table time into a toxic wasteland. It is no respecter of persons and fiercely stands guard during family gatherings.

So I don't have warm, sleepy memories of those events. Tensions ran too high for me to doze off. But as the years went on, something miraculous began to occur. Rusted chains started to loosen. A stubborn old German man, who'd fled his war-torn homeland as a seventeen-year-old boy, began to seek freedom—from himself, his past, his addiction, his shame. This grandpa of mine who'd been bound to the bottle finally found redemption through the Lord Jesus Christ. And ever so slowly, with chains demolished and curses shattered, the family tiptoed down a broken road to rebuilding. Family potlucks symbolized something fresh after that—new beginnings, new recipes, generational transitions.

It's been decades since those early potluck memories were first made, and I've enjoyed hundreds since then, even as my roles have evolved throughout the seasons: from being the diner, to the server, and for the last twenty years, the organizer. The *default* organizer, I might add, for every organization, sports team, social or church group I'm a part of. Because whether I attempt to say no or not—whether I'm present at the planning meeting when the duties are dished out or not—I'm always put in charge of the obligatory potluck meal. The rumors have gotten around that this is my thing. And after decades of diving into this hodgepodge experiment, this culinary and social adventure, I guess they're right. It's worked itself into my muscle memory. The potluck is now second nature to me.

It was no different at a recent year-end basketball banquet. Parents and kids helped roll the round tables into the church gym, unloaded the folding chairs off the cart, and set everything up, leaving a special spot for the long table of honor, where that myriad of sweet and salty pleasures would soon be taking its rightful spot. As I looked around the gym that night, basketball hoops flanked the festivities. Stark white walls encompassed the room. The place was devoid of any ambiance besides the votive candles I'd littered across the dollar store tablecloths.

And yet I was at home. Because wherever an open table is set and my people are gathered . . .

I am home.

There's an unspoken agreement to the potluck: "Even if you're empty-handed, come anyhow. There's room at the table; there's more than enough; we've brought extras just for you." There's also an unspoken assumption: with a table this generous, with a selection this extensive, there's always a little something for everyone. Even the pickiest eaters can find a bit to forage and nibble on.

Or so I thought.

One of the people who showed up at our sports potluck that night, first in line, proved to be the most reluctant diner I'd ever encountered. A teenager who wore his attitude on his sleeve, he swaggered past the chicken casserole, then the fried chicken. He didn't even slow down for the pot roast or the chili, the soup or the salads, the bread or the biscuits—apparently unable to find anything he liked or wanted. And just when I thought he'd finally be tempted by the piping-hot lasagna that oozed with an extra layer of cheese, he kept on going. Walking and looking, examining and ignoring, his plate stayed empty. All the way to the end of the table.

As host, standing by, I wrestled with my inner questions and whether I should try implementing a solution. *Doesn't everyone find something he likes at a potluck? Should I pull the "mom card" and force this high schooler to eat? What can I do to make it more appetizing, more appealing?* My momma's heart wished I could put him in a high chair, pile my favorites onto his plate, and spoon-feed him until I knew he'd received something. But long after he'd wandered away unfed and unimpressed, I still couldn't get him out of my mind.

I realize my first inclination as rescuer and caretaker is just not the way it works sometimes, either at the table or in community. Sometimes people just don't want what we're offering. I try not to get my feelings hurt, but the reality is that no matter what I attempt, they don't like it.

But is the risk of the potluck still worth it? Even if they refuse it? Even if they make us uncomfortable? Should we ever stop inviting? Isn't it easier to keep the guest list limited to people who will be grateful and appreciate the experience? Do we spoil our fun and fellowship by risking conversations that might challenge our faith a bit, that might create opportunities where we need to love through our differences?

Jesus once told a story that reveals His heart of hospitality, how He yearns for a table where all are represented and welcomed.

"A man was giving a large banquet and invited many. At the time of the banquet, he sent his servant to tell those who were invited, 'Come, because everything is now ready.'

"But without exception they all began to make excuses. The first one said to him, 'I have bought a field, and I must go out and see it. I ask you to excuse me.'

"Another said, 'I have bought five yoke of oxen, and I'm going to try them out. I ask you to excuse me.'

"And another said, 'I just got married, and therefore I'm unable to come.'

"So the servant came back and reported these things to his master. Then in anger, the master of the house told his servant, 'Go out quickly into the streets and alleys of the city, and bring in here the poor, maimed, blind, and lame.'

'Master,' the servant said, 'what you ordered has been done, and there's still room.'

"Then the master told the servant, 'Go out into the highways and hedges and make them come in, so that my house may be filled.'" (Luke 14:16–23)

Our potluck, our table—if we want to model it after the heart of Jesus—should get us creative with our invitations. Whenever we widen the communal circle of the potluck, whether by planned intention or as a result of unexpected circumstances, it makes wiggle room for everyone, especially those who've never been included on our guest list before. Only by extending the boundaries to welcome more variety and diversity into our midst do we begin to unearth the uniqueness others bring to the conversation. By widening the table to a wealth of new discoveries and shared perspectives, that's how we most vividly reflect the true kingdom of God and function as the whole body of Christ.

But while beautiful in theory, while nice to think about and aspire toward, this is where things start to get messy, right? There's a reason we like to stick with what's comfortable. There's a reason we prefer sharing the table with people who look, talk, work, and live the same way we do. We prefer the safety, the sameness, the simple because it all adds up to security.

But that's a total lie. Because following Jesus means getting dirty, getting risky. Following Jesus means asking and inviting. Following Jesus means hanging around with people who aren't our kind of people.

Following Jesus means crossing boundaries and cultural divides—social, racial, political, and more—knowing this is the essence of the gospel. As Paul reminds us, "Welcome one another as Christ has welcomed you, for the glory of God" (Rom. 15:7 ESV). Only as we listen to what others are really saying, even those with whom we disagree, and by developing real relationships with those who are vastly different from us can we begin to address the misperceptions that persist about Christian faith and the church. I know the truth of this, but let's be heart honest: the kinds of people Jesus hung around with on a regular basis aren't the people with whom I'd choose to hang.

Think of who was on Jesus' invite list. Pharisees, fishermen, tax collectors. The deformed, the sick, the adulterers, the homeless, the refugees, the wanderers, the possessed, even the unclean. Risky individuals, all of them. Yet He wasn't afraid of interacting with any of them. And neither should we be. We need to get up from our safe, anonymous distance behind our heated Facebook debates and our opinionated rants and actually live like Jesus lived.

Get messy. Be real. Stir up your guest lists, instead of stirring the pot.

Our table, like Jesus' table, should be one that offers radical, even scandalous grace. To all. To anyone.

I don't mean, of course, in our desire to love and welcome others, that we compromise the truth of the gospel with something more palatable, not wanting to offend. I'm just saying we too often come to a diverse table with an agenda, rather than with humble hearts wanting to hear. Instead of asking thoughtful questions, we attack. Rather than listening, we implode. And when others don't agree with us, we no longer extend the invitation.

How can we ever share effectively Christ's message of peace, reconciliation, forgiveness, and love if our table is closed to those Jesus welcomed? To those He invited? To those who, like us, are broken and in need of a Savior?

When we grow in our opportunities to love through differences, we proclaim God's goodness to those who observe it, and we set a table that surprises all with the freedom it represents.

So, will we choose to be counted within the company of Jesus' dinner party—as one of the outcasts He invited—or will we choose to eat only at the special table reserved for those who appear to have it all together? We have a choice. The pretty, polished, seemingly perfect dinner guest is an awfully safe and comfortable companion, and that's who I've been drawn toward more often than not. But I'm thinking that when we kick comfort to the curb, our table overflows to look a whole lot more like Jesus' table did.

Yikes, I know that's convicting. If not to you, it sure is to me because words are easy, but the implementation? Not so much. This whole concept of throwing open the invitation is risky. Honestly, putting radical love into action makes me all sweaty and nervous, but I've begun to ask the question: "Who is missing at my table?" Am I willing to enlarge the boundaries of my heart to allow the core of gospel living to include anyone and everyone? Does my table look like Jesus' table, set for all who are hungry and in need? Yes, I know there's risk, but the rewards are worth it. For as I extend an invitation to come to the potluck, as I pull up another chair and add another leaf, I can feel my heart opening up as well. The only alternative, really, by polarizing those around me, is to end up looking less like Christ than those who don't even know Him.

I think back to the sports banquet potluck and to our reluctant diner who refused what we offered him. Know why he did? Because he's difficult. Because he's challenging. Because he's complicated. And because we have to work harder to satisfy him.

Let me tell you what I know about this guy. Our daughter and our nephew first met him at the YMCA, where most people saw him as a bad influence, a loner. But our kids started inviting him to shoot baskets with them before they went in to work out. And as each shot went up, he'd share a bit more of his story. Over the weeks they learned he'd been kicked out of multiple schools—the last offense being so grievous no school would admit him again. He was lost. Still is. And the statistics are stacked against him.

This young man's been pushed away from almost all the tables in his life. No one really wants him at theirs. Life is easier that way, but we invited him to our table anyhow . . . because that's the heart of Jesus, because that's the spirit of the gospel. And because that's the rewarding possibility of the potluck.

Two years have passed since that first invitation. We still can't force him to partake, but the welcome always stands. Sometimes he accepts; sometimes he doesn't.

But if *our* table isn't open, whose will be?

Dear Jen

I don't know where to start with extending an invitation to someone different from me. I don't want to force something that might seem awkward.

Uncomfortable

Dear Uncomfortable,

We must always remember it's about doing authentic community with people, not checking off an expected to-do list.

If you have children, might I suggest beginning with them? Some of the most special and diverse groups of friends we've gotten to know have come through our sons' sports teams and the local school. When one of our boys became aware of those around him who didn't have much to eat, I began packing extras into his lunch for him to share. He reached out to those sitting by themselves and began unofficially mentoring a few underclassmen who needed someone in their corner. Our kids can often be an open door to relationship that would otherwise be shut in our face. We need to intentionally seek out those opportunities.

Contact area ministries that focus on displaced refugees or the homeless. As we've welcomed them around our table, our eyes have been opened and our prejudices defused. We've asked questions, learned their stories, and realized how quickly people's lives can change, often by circumstances out of their control.

Reach out to a neighboring church of different demographics. Our church is passionately trying to break down the walls that keep us from interacting more freely with other believers. We recently had a combined worship service with a sister congregation. Together we created a diverse mingling of races and backgrounds. The time we spent in worship, confession, and sharing Communion together was phenomenal, and the conversations around the table were both eye-opening and enriching.

Or be honest and reach out to someone totally different from you and acknowledge to them, "I want to do something to bring unity to our diverse community. Would you be interested in joining me?" What's the worst they can say?

Jen

Elevate the Ordinary

❀ Are you ready for the risk and reward of a potluck? I rarely host a meal where guests don't bring something to share, so I've mastered the perfectly imperfect potluck. These are my best tips to help you do the same.

1. Learn to let go.

I know you envision a perfectly planned menu, but flexibility is key. People typically have a favorite recipe they like to bring, and allowing guests to choose their own contribution makes it more enjoyable for them as well. If your potluck is a smaller gathering, however, you'll want to assign basic menu items so dinner doesn't include three pasta salads. (Ask me how I know.)

2. Plan the menu.

When I host a potluck at home, I always provide the main dish because it guarantees we're not snacking on hummus, carrots, and cheesecake all evening. If it's at another location, like a tailgate, I also provide all the paper products and necessary utensils. Communicate what everyone is bringing. When I plan our large potluck meals for 50–150 people, I send around a Word document or use a group organizing website like SignUpGenius.com to ensure all categories are covered. Even so, I always stress that this is a general guideline and that not signing up shouldn't keep anyone from coming.

3. Prepare to care for your guests' needs.

People always forget things, so make sure you've pulled out extra serving spoons, serving knives, hot pads, and even spatulas beforehand. Also provide easy access to platters, bowls, and baskets. Have pens, note cards, or cute little chalkboard tags available so guests can write down the name of the dish and include any necessary information, such as "vegetarian," "spicy," "gluten free," or "contains nuts." A fun twist is to use butcher paper instead of a tablecloth. That way, in lieu of note cards, guests can write their description right on the paper.

4. Always have extra.

Nothing makes a host (or guest) panic more than looking around at the food offerings and realizing there's not enough to eat. After planning dozens of casual potlucks, I've learned the secret through trial and error. Always plan to provide more food than you think you need. I always have hot dogs (if kids are part of the event), as well as a box of angel hair noodles and a jar of red sauce waiting in the wings. Thin noodles cook up in five minutes, giving you a pasta dish you can add quickly to the table if more food is needed. If all else fails, pizza is always the answer.

EXTRA HELPING *from my brother Steve*

The Pineapple Place

We don't let hospitality be controlled by a "when, then" mentality: *when* we have this or that, *then* we can practice hospitality. We've simply done what we can with what we've had and watched God work in and through us for His purposes.

When my wife, Susie, and I moved into our first house, we made it a priority to add a guest area in the basement as soon as resources allowed. Our kids quickly embraced and looked forward to the opportunities to have others live with us for whatever period of time they needed. Even in this season, the four boys shared a 10 x 10-foot room, and the four girls shared a 10 x 12-foot room to keep the basement available for guests.

With the addition onto our house, we launched into a new chapter in our hospitality outreach. Driven by the idea of having a place for out-of-town family and a place of refuge for missionaries on furlough, we turned the space on top of our detached garage into what we called "the Pineapple Place."

We named this new addition as we did for two reasons: (1) the pine-apple is the international symbol for hospitality, and (2) we had been greatly impacted by missionary Otto Koning's book *The Pineapple Story* and the necessity of yielding our rights for the benefit to others. We invested in the Pineapple Place so that those the Lord brought through its doors would feel welcomed and could refresh and replenish as they felt necessary. The separate building gave them the option of engaging with our family or spending time alone.

The ways our lives have been enriched by those God has sent our way are too numerous to count, especially as the generational impact has yet to be fully seen through the lives of our eight kids practicing their forms of hospitality. We cherish the memories already made and look forward to the new ones that are still to come.

The diversity of people God has brought into our lives from around the world is amazing as we stay receptive to requests, not proactive in seeking tenants. Here are a few of them, referenced by the countries they're from or the countries to which they are ministering:

- *Guinea West Africa.* This family was one of the key motivators to create the Pineapple Place. Coincidentally, we later found out the father of this family was the son of my fifth-grade teacher, who was my all-time favorite teacher!
- *Australia.* This pastor of a western Australia church had a congregation that consisted of farmers with an average farm size of forty square miles.
- *Papua New Guinea.* This young couple with three young children needed a place to recuperate after a difficult departure from the field.
- *Russia/China.* The wife was from China and arrived eight-plus months pregnant. She did not know anyone in America besides her in-laws.
- *India.* These lifetime missionary mentors were working to encourage other missionaries as they go through the trials of their callings.
- *Ghana.* This family established an orphanage for unwanted children in the capital city, most of whom have significant physical challenges.
- *Germany, Russia, Israel.* Friends and coworkers of one of our children spent sixteen months on a cross-cultural mission project.
- *Tajikistan/Indonesia.* The husband in this family was training to be a pilot for Mission Aviation Fellowship.
- *Afghanistan/Turkey.* The Pineapple Place was a quiet place for a young family to recover after having to leave their work without notice due to terrorist danger.
- *Egypt.* A leader of the evangelical church in Egypt had to flee for his personal safety after three attempts were made on his life.
- *Northern Africa.* This man was living as a nomad to minister to the nomadic people of the region.

- *Bible Quiz Teams.* These youth ministry teams came from around the country.
- *Workers of our home remodel.* Many of them were with us for most of the entire project.
- *Many, many friends (and sometimes strangers).* Our kids brought people home with them—often without first asking for permission—because they knew our door was always open to others.

I'm grateful to my parents for modeling what it means to be available to meet the needs of others and building a legacy of hospitality that we've been able to continue and pass down to our children. We are blessed to echo the sentiments of Psalm 115:1: "Not to us, LORD, not to us, but to your name give glory because of your faithful love, because of your truth."

10

Come as You Are

As my hospitality has expanded over the years, I've learned to be a place (both my home as well as my heart) that announces, "Your brokenness is welcome. Your questions, anger, and frustration are welcome. Your loneliness and hurt are welcome here. Your desperation and doubt are okay." It's evolved with time, but I've worked really hard at doing that—at giving people a safe landing spot where they can take a deep breath and give themselves permission to acknowledge, "I don't have my *act* together, but I still want to *be* together."

I'm still learning, though, the humility it takes to *receive* this kind of hospitality.

This revelation came home to me not long ago while I was racing the clock against the weight of a huge obligation and book deadline. I hadn't left the house in a week. Laundry was piled everywhere. Healthy vegetables had become a foreign concept. I'd been living off caffeine and nutty bars (no judgment, please). By week's end I was wearing the same clothes I'd slept in, sporting three-day hair, and didn't even care.

And in that moment the doorbell rang. Oh, yes, it did.

Did I stop, drop, and roll to avoid this unexpected drop-in? Nope, couldn't really get away with that—not after I'd just spent sixty thousand words elevating the importance of living a life of welcome, of choosing to open the door during even the most inconvenient of times.

But, oh, those poor people, whoever they were. They had no idea what was about to greet them.

I peeked through the window, only to find two of my best friends, Gina and Georgia, standing there smiling, holding Starbucks treats and fresh fruit. (They would have brought my favorite food, French fries,

I'm sure, but they knew I needed vitamins.) And though I never, ever do this, ever—ever!—

I sobbed.

Like a full-blown, shoulders-heaving cry.

Growing up with three older brothers who played pranks and practical jokes as if it was their spiritual gift, I developed a kind of bootstraps mentality. You take it in stride; you keep going. So unless probed—unless you *really* want to know—I tend to be a silent sufferer. That's why, since I hadn't reached out for support, everyone assumed I was doing fine. They had no idea how overwhelmed I was, that I'd been in so deep, swimming so long underwater, it hadn't crossed my mind to send out a much-needed SOS. What I *did* send out, in fact—as cover, I guess—was a celebratory comment on Facebook mentioning my excitement about being almost done with this book deadline, which most people received as cause for congratulating me.

But not these two besties—the ones who really know me—who could read between the lines and hear my heart crying out, "I haven't left my house all week!" They knew isolation plus Jen Schmidt did not equal "I'm fine."

Speaking of—can I cut away here for a second and talk about the real trouble I've got with "How are you? I'm fine"? Unfortunately, we've become a society where "How are you?" is a rhetorical question people don't really want anyone to answer. It's become our cultural head nod. In fact, when my parents host international students and give them a list of idioms unique to American slang, they explain that "How are you?" is basically the same as "Hi," so that if someone asks "How are you?" without stopping for an answer, don't be offended. That's a sad societal standard.

As is "fine." We can eat fine food. We can enjoy fine cars. We can dress ourselves up in fine clothes, but to always be "fine" doesn't cut it anymore in my friendships. Fine is for china, which most of us haven't used in decades (except for my tea parties), so why start now? I don't do superficial well, and I've stopped even using the word *fine*. Ask me how I'm doing, and my answer will probably be polite. But it won't be "fine."

Rant over.

So as I was saying . . . my ambassadors of hope had known there was nothing "fine" in the sound of my online voice or my invisible body language. And as soon as they walked through that door, all my emotions, exhaustion, and stress, stirred and shaken with profound gratitude, welled up at once and poured out in tears. I stood there in my yoga pants and coffee-stained shirt with my three-day hair (okay, four-day hair) while they reminded me to breathe and assured me I was going to be all right. The finish line can be close and yet feel so far away, and they knew I needed someone else to tell me I was almost done.

Gina and Georgia are two of my "come as you are" friends. I only have a few of them—the kind of friends who see right through any faking fine. We've seen one another through sickness, aging parents, unemployment, and suspicious lumps. We've cried tears of disappointment during loss and identified with broken dreams. We've laughed so hard until tears ran down onto our legs. We've gathered around the casket of a mother and mourned desperately for what should have been. We've danced at the weddings of one another's children—the same ones whose diapers we've changed—and we've celebrated through job promotions, scholarships, and fun getaways. They've hurt my feelings. I've hurt theirs. But through it all we've fought for our friendship. We've fought past the "fine" to create spaces where we can each lay our whole-hearted selves down. We've allowed the imperfections of our friendship to strengthen us. A sisterhood of the imperfect.

But to get to that place is risky—like the potluck is risky. It means mustering up a lot of bravery when you don't feel it and showing up for the everyday. Advancing when you feel like retreating. Investing when you feel like withdrawing. But it's what leads to things like two dear friends taking their hospitality on the go, bringing it to my front door, becoming that safe place for me, right when I needed it.

That's the message I want to live, and that's the invitation I want to extend. The most profound gift of friendship and hospitality we can give is the assurance, "You are welcome exactly the way you are, and you are worth showing up for." It's the Jesus way. The risky, relentless, and scandalous way. The gift of grace given without expectation of anything in return.

"Come as you are."

"Come as you are" is an invitation I've extended on my blog for years. When you're known for freely sharing your bedlam moments—those messy, less-than-perfect moments—you start a mini revolution of women who need a place for theirs. (Everyone has them. It's only whether or not you're willing to share them.)

As a result, I get the most hilarious e-mails, texts, and pictures of crazy things that other women know I'll appreciate—odd stories of conversation bloopers, a dinner casserole that exploded on the ceiling, kids who wipe unmentionables on the walls next to their cribs, women who find something hilarious in a thrift store, and pictures of messy houses. (Lots of messy houses.) Sometimes the stories are even laced with such bravery amid their great pain because women know I'll also understand that too. Incredible freedom comes in sharing those things, both the sidesplitting and the heartrending. It's a glimpse of what I want for this sisterhood of imperfect women.

Honestly, you can't make this stuff up. In fact, here's one I witnessed myself—another delightful episode of "Come as You Are."

On a beautiful spring day, families gathered in our backyard for a cookout. My friend Bonnie had brought a unique fruit salad to contribute to the cookout. Kind of fruity, mainly dessert—we couldn't figure out exactly what category to place it in. It was so yummy, and I told her I needed that recipe.

"Oh, it's so easy," she replied, with a self-deprecating laugh—"so easy that we made it in the backseat while we were driving here."

My mouth dropped open. *What?* I had to know the rest of the story. When you thrive on authenticity like I do, sometimes a simple question releases the floodgates for something even better.

She whispered how they'd had no time to make anything, but she didn't want to come empty-handed. So she piled all the ingredients in the van, brought a huge mixing bowl, and honestly made it while they were driving—spatula and all. "Well, actually I told my ten-year-old daughter how to make it, just so you don't think I was a distracted driver."

Imagining the hilarity of it, I grabbed my friend in a bear hug and exclaimed, "Bonnie, I love you now more than ever. This is my kind of bedlam. Can we please tell the other ladies your story?"

Nervous that they'd think she was crazy, she finally gave in. I can be relentless.

After her comedic rendition of how they popped pineapple cans, dumped whip cream, mixed pudding, and added fruit, all in the van, we doubled over in laughter. This is what the sisterhood of imperfect friendship is all about—sharing simple moments that women are often too afraid to admit.

Then she volunteered one other detail that opened her "come as you are" heart even further. Embarrassed that people might see inside her van, she admitted that she'd parked up our driveway so no one would walk past.

"Wait," I inquired, "you mean it's all still in your van? All the stuff you used to make it?"

"Oh, yes."

Together we walked our long gravel drive. I had to see it to believe it (and photograph it, of course). And there in the back seat of her minivan, filled with dirty bowls, remnants of whipped cream, spatulas covered in pudding, and empty fruit cans, I witnessed the most delightful symbolism of sisterhood. Chaos, mess, imperfection, flexibility, and leftovers, all mixed together to make something strikingly sweet and beautiful. A vision representing where life-on-life meets the nitty-gritty. And trust me, the proof is in the pudding. (The pictures and evidence are on my blog.)

Bonnie's hilarious vulnerability opened up the conversation to many other stories that evening, both funny and heartfelt. It took only one person willing to unveil her story first to find out it didn't serve as a noose. It became instead a bridge, a visible gift to all those wondering if they were the only one.

That's become my hosting philosophy behind what's now come to be known as my "Come as You Are" nights.

The first one I hosted, I did it sort of accidentally. It started out as a get-together for young moms from our church, but I'd overloaded my schedule that week, and I was exhausted. (When will I learn that activity doesn't equal maturity, that a busy life is not a badge of honor?) Still, I knew I wanted to gather with these sweet ladies and share a bit of my heart, but I didn't want the pressure of deep-dive cleaning—or *any* cleaning, for that matter (except the bathroom; that's a must). Nor did I want to put on my cute boots or fix my hair, and honestly the thought of chasing the Web for some great recipe to test out was a deal breaker too. I had nothing to prove, so here was my humble invitation as their church mentor mom:

"Ladies, this is a 'Come as You Are' night."

I was throwing the expectation of perfection out the window. "Come as you are with whatever clothes you'd ordinarily put on after a long, hard day of work. I'm assuming that's sweatpants, PJs, no shower, doesn't matter. *(When I talked to the ladies separately, I inserted "bras optional.")* You can bring food if you want, but you don't have to. All failed Pinterest recipes welcome. No using stoves allowed, half-eaten bags of chips encouraged, and if you don't bring anything, that's perfect too. (Unless your love language is homemade chocolate chip cookies, then go for it. I'd hate to rob you of that blessing. Ha!)"

And that's exactly how they came—in slippers, in sweatpants, in T-shirts and tanks, with unwashed hair and unwashed hearts. And it started something so beautiful we never wanted the night to end.

After food and coffee and sweet tea and sodas, I gathered everyone in the family room, and we snuggled on the sofas, as well as on the floor. I brought out every pillow and fuzzy blanket I owned (even bought a few extras for good measure), and I spread them out for everyone to grab. I wanted this to be a safe haven for open conversation, and being cuddled up in a cozy blanket is a perfect start. It helps rip away the pretenses. The gift of hospitality is meant to create more than just warm, welcoming spaces, but ones that ensure safety.

Then here's pretty much what I said. Maybe it'll help you as you think about hosting these kinds of gatherings yourself.

One of the greatest gifts you can give one another, ladies, is your imperfection. Our stories are gifts we must share. We must wrestle past the *fine*, dive deep into real life, let go of others' expectations, and allow our authenticity to bond our community.

As Christians, we're not very good at this. We're happy sharing the hope, glory, and grace of Christ, but to share our struggles is difficult. Yet sharing our mess unwraps the hidden gem of our message. When we tear down walls and acknowledge our need for grace in our hard moments, His name is elevated. Jesus used stories to connect with us throughout Scripture. Sharing our stories can point to Him.

"So I'm making clear right now," I continued, "this is a safe place to share. I will not betray confidences, I will uphold your reputation, and I ask the rest of you to do the same." We'd all agreed to "come as we are," and I wanted everyone glad they did, wanting to come back again soon without fear or judgment. "But as the Queen of Forced Bonding, I'm going to ask you some questions."

A few eye rolls and a little nervous laughter swept through the room.

I know, I know. If you'd thought there was homework, you might not have come, but it'll be worth it. It gives us an opportunity to get to know one another better and connect on a deeper level.

Most of you know one another. But first, tell us all a bit about your family. Then, share one "Mom Win" and one "Mom Fail" from the week. I realize it's easy to think of a roll call full of ways we're failing as moms. Some of them you might not feel like admitting. But as we share a "fail," it pulls down a wall and gives a glimpse into our heart about those things with which we're struggling.

What's hardest sometimes is to find that one "win"—a seemingly unimportant thing to celebrate, a reason to choose gratitude in the midst of a really difficult day. But I think we need to seek it out and name it. It matters. We need to be women who celebrate one another. It's also a way to share something encouraging without feeling like we're bragging about one of our children. It gives us a chance to celebrate a hard-won moment.

After explaining the "win" and "fail" model, which includes the delicate balance between vulnerability and not oversharing personal information about others, I volunteered to go first. Because honestly, there's a gift in having a friend willing to go first, to dive deep and pull back the layers. It gave me the opportunity to model deeper, more authentic conversations—although actually, it didn't take much on my part for some pretty special things to start happening.

Lots of heavy hearts were revealed, as well as encouraging moments of God's faithfulness. See if you recognize yourself in any of these cries that were shared in that sacred "come as you are" space. (See, you're not alone.)

> "What does going deep and discipling my ten-year-old child even look like? I don't know what that means on a day-to-day basis—especially because my husband has turned his back on our faith. He's not really even present anymore, but our kids still need their daddy."

> "I can't find a 'win' this week. I honestly have no idea." *(Tears began to flow.)* "My husband has had a huge job transition, and it's as if he's going through a midlife crisis at thirty-two. Is that even possible?"

> "I'm so lonely. How can I be lonely when I'm surrounded by my kids all day? Please tell me I'm not the only one."

> "I love my kids so much, but right now I don't like my daughter at all." *(Tears streamed again as we all nodded our heads.)* "As a mom, can I even admit that? I don't like my own kid? She's often hard to like. Have I done something wrong? Have I dropped the ball?"

> "I'm embarrassed by mine too," another mom chimed in. "And then the Lord reminds me of my own wretched heart. And yet He's come for *us* because of His love for *us*."

> "Have you ever heard a banshee yell? Have you? Because that was me. I didn't know sounds like that could be uttered by the human voice. Before kids I didn't even think I *had* a temper."

"Angry mom here too," another said. Five others raised their hands. "Me too. Angry mom." Again, heads nodded in understanding.

Continuing around the circle, what began as a short exercise stretched to hours, punctuated at repeated intervals by the women saying how much they all needed an evening like this. As I listened to these precious young moms chasing hard after God, wanting to go deep for their families, willing to fight for their marriages, I saw in them an understanding that life isn't always *fine* and that it's never meant to be done alone. And in those places where they were hurting the most, I saw the Lord come "near the brokenhearted," ministering His strength to "those crushed in spirit" (Ps. 34:18).

As we finished, a mom who'd done her sharing earlier in the evening wiped her eyes and raised her hand with a chuckle, "Uh, I think I should get to go again because I would share something a lot more personal this time around. I went first, and then you guys brought down the walls." *Exactly.* It was one of those all too rare nights in her life where she'd been given permission to go deep. Vulnerability had led to transparency, which led to hearts of empathy. And by the end of the night as we closed in prayer and Scripture, we were all changed.

We'd come as we are.

We were leaving as new people.

So, what do you think? How would you like to be part of bringing this kind of healing, conviction, and life change to others as you open your door and as God works through you? I for one know *I* want to do it more often and more effectively, and I imagine you feel the same way.

Many women, when they get to talking about hospitality at this much deeper, more vulnerable level, share their fears with me about hosting, especially in terms of how to facilitate conversation—the way I've described in this chapter. That's a real concern. Yet just as you can learn to become more comfortable with hosting over time, learning to take conversations to the next level is a skill you can learn as well. Both become more natural as you execute them. So let me encourage you . . .

Depend on the Lord. We pursue hospitality from that deep, spiritual well that's filled only by Him. Vulnerability serves as the truest gateway to community, as well as to real and abiding friendships. So since the desire of the "come as you are" host is to invite relationships that pass through the superficial and become more transparent, let it start with you. Share your story because it's really His story. If you're not yet at the place where you feel comfortable hosting and leading, ask a friend who facilitates conversations easily to host with you and help direct the flow of the evening. There's nothing wrong with asking. If you're willing and ready to take the first step, deeper relationships will occur as you get out of your comfort zone. By depending on Him, you'll discover He even cares about things like meaningful conversations and will help you grow in leading them. Be the first to "come as you are," knowing that Christ is enough and that we are enough through Him.

Follow up on your desire. If you're anything like me, you feel as though superficial chitchat needed to end at about the eighth grade. You feel like, if you're going to take the time to invest in radical hospitality, you want it to count for kingdom purpose, right? So from this starting point, you're already at the right place to invite the weary, the messy, the brokenhearted, and the questioning to come and find rest. As the host, seek to create an environment that makes it okay not to be okay. When Jesus gathered people, He used that time to share some of the most profound truths of the gospel. Think of your conversations as offering a cross-shaped welcome to others, becoming the conduit by which hospitality and the gospel intersect.

Honestly, it happens as you do it. Gina and Georgia, for instance, simply stepped out there and rang my doorbell. And because they did, they impacted my life at a deeper level than they could have imagined. When they left, I was still wearing the same frumpy clothes, still facing the same challenges, still sitting in the same spot. But after I'd received their grace and encouragement, after I'd eaten the fruit and the treats, and after I'd rewarmed the coffee in my microwave (twice!), my heart was alive, renewed, refreshed.

We get to play a small part in this most glorious opportunity of declaring that He welcomes us just as we are. Welcome others with that same dependent, trusting, open, and vulnerable heart, and you'll see your desire for authenticity come to life. It's not easy, but it's always worth it.

Dear Jen

I get nervous thinking about keeping the conversation going, especially around a more formal dinner-table situation. What if there are awkward silences? What if we don't click in conversation?

At a Loss for Words

Dear At a Loss,

I promise this is a skill you can learn. So much of it begins by showing interest in your guest, in knowing how to ask good questions and then learning to listen well.

Questions show humility. It means you want the focus directed at others and not on yourself. Questions give everyone a voice. As a host, you'll find the trickiest part is learning to graciously interrupt and steer the conversation so that everyone is included. Here are a few tips:

- Have a few conversation starter questions ready in case you run out of ideas and find a lull in the conversation. Make sure they're open-ended questions. Yes-or-no questions are immediate conversation killers.
- A fun game I've used with all ages is letting a prepicked penny spark conversation. Have a jar full of pennies on the table. Each guest picks one, reads the year that's inscribed on it, and then shares a memory or something significant that happened to her in that year.
- Whenever guests answer with brevity, I've learned to urge people to continue their story by saying, "That's so interesting. I'd love to hear more." Or, "Can you elaborate on that? What did you learn from . . . ? How did you feel when . . . ?" This keeps the conversation going and lets your guests know you're still engaged.

For deeper level connections Jesus is my model. He posed questions to get to the heart. Do you realize when He asked them, He didn't need an answer? He already knew the answer, yet He guided the questions with skilled purpose, always leading people to dive deeper into spiritual truths. Sometimes He used open-ended questions that got people to think more deeply. But often He shot back with direct questions that sliced straight through pharisaical religious talk. As I learn from His questioning skills and attempt to apply them to my own relationships, they always expose a new layer of understanding. He brings about discovery and encourages us to mull over truths that always point back to the gospel.

Jen

Elevate the Ordinary

❀ Do you need a reminder of how much your Father loves you and pursues you? Write out the truth of His Word: I am loved. I am chosen. I am called. I am redeemed. I am worthy. I am accepted. And then remind a friend of the same (maybe along with some coffee?).

❀ As every family member walks through the door today, greet them with a "come as you are" welcome. They may think you've lost it, but life is short, and they need to feel extra loved today. So celebrate them like they've been gone from you. If you're not expecting anyone, put that same kind of celebration toward a special friend.

❀ Start creating your own "Come as You Are" guest list. Grab your calendar, pick a date, and determine now—no more procrastinating. You won't regret it.

11

Elephant in the Room

*W*hat is the instruction that wise ol' grannies used to give us? "Never bring up a woman's age, her weight, or how much money she makes."

And yet I say, What better place than right here to break all the rules and speak to the largest hospitality elephant in the room.

Cold, hard cash.

Many women voice resistance to opening their home due to budgetary limitations. They've resigned themselves to believing that a beautiful welcome must include grand gestures that require an even larger pocketbook. I'm here to tell you, however, this is simply not true.

The reason I can talk so confidently on this subject is because it doesn't feel so long ago that our life felt hard, suffocating. A time when we went nearly a year without a paycheck. We were trying to keep a business afloat and were committed to paying our employees first. But for us, it meant barely being able to pay our own bills as a family of six (then) and stretching our budget so thinly that I was practically snapping pennies in two.

In the midst of all this—in addition to the financial strain—my young, vibrant mother-in-law had been diagnosed with a brain tumor and given only months to live. Just a year prior, my thirty-four-year-old sister-in-law had passed away from breast cancer, leaving my brother widowed with three precious young children. We were still reeling from that too. Life was bearing down on me from all directions, and I felt like I could hardly breathe.

I begged God for clarity but heard nothing. I cried out, wondering how much longer this season would last, but no answers were forthcoming. I clung to Jesus' promise, how "in this world you will have trouble.

But take heart! I have overcome the world" (John 16:33 NIV). Still, I can't tell you how often my grip came close to slipping.

And yet in those dire moments, hospitality became a lifeline.

I'll admit, my tired self was really tempted to close the door to others and hunker down with my family. I'm sure people would have understood my decision to retreat and seek rest. (There's nothing wrong with that.) But even as things went south, we continued to host our Friday evening small group for couples with kids. We all pitched in a few dollars for a babysitter, who played with the children upstairs so we could have our Bible time downstairs. Everyone brought a snack to share, and I provided the cheapest of all: homemade popcorn. We definitely had no money for making it pretty and impressive, and no one expected it. All we had to offer was ourselves, bare-bones as it was.

But looking back sixteen years later with the hindsight and deepened wisdom forged through difficulties, I don't know how we (or any of us) would have survived if we'd tried going it alone. Because week after week, life went from bad to worse. The dreaded updates kept rolling in. Our prayer requests turned into prayer pleadings.

Not only was our own company continuing its decline, but another group member lost his job; a dad died unexpectedly; my mother-in-law passed away within a month of her diagnosis; one couple began struggling in their marriage; another had lost all control with their kids. It was all too much. At times, I felt downright angry and frustrated, broken and spent. But still we kept opening up our home, we kept coming together as a small group, and we kept taking turns pointing one another to the cross. We honestly acknowledged, "Life stinks right now, but God is good, all the time." We supported one another, checked in on one another, and found reasons to keep laughing, even if sometimes we just sat in silence and listened.

But here's what I'm saying: When things felt completely out of my control and I had no answers, I was forced to choose. Declare His promises or disappear into my doubt. Avoid doing life in community and the vulnerability that comes along with it, or wrestle my spirit to find ways to bring Him glory in the midst of it. I needed to stay committed to opening my life up to others—actively loving God and loving my neighbor—even when I didn't feel like it. Even when I couldn't afford it.

I thought a lot about hospitality during that year. Sometimes we don't understand radical hospitality until we experience it with completely empty hands. When all has been stripped away and we've cried out to the only One who can fill them, He shifts our perspective. He shows us why continuing to offer what little we can bring is such a vital part of living in community, of creating opportunities for showing to others and receiving ourselves the faithfulness and generosity of God.

Nothing else can explain what happened—again, about a full year into living off our savings, selling items for cash, and then dipping into debt—when I came home from a long, tiring day running errands with our four preschool kids. I approached our side door, wearily hauling the infant carrier over one arm, and . . .

I couldn't believe what I was seeing. Brown paper bags lined our sidewalk, each of them stuffed with pure manna: food, toiletries, diapers, gift cards, all overflowing from a row of grocery sacks left for my family, accompanied only by unsigned notes of love and encouragement.

I don't know how many Scripture promises He seemed to fulfill for me in that one moment: "Those who sow in tears will reap with shouts of joy" (Ps. 126:5). "Weeping may endure for a night, but joy comes in the morning" (Ps. 30:5 NKJV). "Greater is He who is in you than he who is in the world" (1 John 4:4 NASB). "Jesus Christ is the same yesterday, today, and forever" (Heb. 13:8). His life-giving water poured over me, disguised as free jugs of milk and cleaning supplies. And as it did, the waterworks exploded. Our babies grabbed hold of my legs, "Mommy, what's wrong. Are you okay?"

"Yes, I sure am," I said, hugging them, smearing my wet cheeks on theirs. "These are happy tears because God sent special angels to share their treats with us."

And it didn't stop there. In addition to the groceries, an envelope showed up in our mailbox a month later with no return address, containing a cashier's check for $100, equally anonymous. Once again these friends who extended hospitality to us when we most needed it expected nothing in return, only that all adulation go to the One worthy of true praise.

In times like these our empty hands, raised palms up to Him, came from hearts begging Him not to waste our pain. I pleaded to Him, "Use it for You, Lord," and He did. He always does. While it was uncomfortable for me and embarrassing to be in this position of need, all He asked was that I receive . . . just as all He'd asked was for me to bring Him my humble offering of hospitality, despite our lack.

Because isn't giving glory to God the goal of everything anyway? And do we really make ourselves any richer by not giving of ourselves?

One of the unique opportunities we miss if we allow money to stand between us and an open-door lifestyle is our children's specific recognition of God as provider and supplier. It's a chance for their appreciation (and mine) to grow for the little things we previously wouldn't even have noticed.

During this time of financial hardship, I coined the phrase "God Watch" for our family. I even spray-painted it on a boulder in our woods, marking that year as a time when our eyes should be especially open to His goodness and generosity. I never wanted to forget—and I never wanted *them* to forget—how the Lord showed up over and over again amid those dark hours, especially when doubt crept so subtly into the crevices of my heart.

It began as a game of sorts for the kids, then morphed into our mantra—an intentional way to actively and purposely watch and wait with an expectant heart for all the ways the Lord would amaze us during such particularly difficult circumstances.

"Our 'God Watch,'" I wrote in a blog post at the time, "is a reminder to gaze at His goodness. To seek it. To rest in His reassurances. To affirm it. But more importantly, it's a whisper of willingness to choose joy in the midst of doubt. To live it." We were seeking out His goodness when we didn't feel it.

But even while wanting to impress this truth on my children's hearts, God used their childlike faith to build my own. Their fervent desire to find God in all the unlikely places spurred unexpected gratitude in all of us, the kind that kept us wanting to reach out to others regardless of our lack of resources. We learned a lot during this time about the difference between needs and wants.

And for a long time afterward, the lessons kept coming.

After seventeen years in our home—this house where we've lived with now *five* children, as well as dogs and cats tearing up the same worn carpet and the same ripped vinyl floors—one of my favorite flooring brands invited me into a blog partnership to replace those nasty things (the floors, not the kids).

Sure, it was an absolute *want*, not a *need*. But since we're committed to paying cash for these types of purchases, it felt like a hug from above. It skyrocketed this rather superficial home improvement project from the bottom of our to-do list right to the top.

When they told me they wanted our flooring done within two weeks—*two weeks!*—I spent the next few days pondering all the laminate and hardwood flooring choices. Wow, I had no idea there were so many options. How does one make such first-world decisions? Dreams of sleek floors filled my thoughts, how I would no longer need to strategically position our furniture over nail polish spills, coffee stains, and thin carpet patches.

As I shared my plans during an extended family gathering I was hosting, one of our relatives exclaimed her excitement. "I am so thrilled for you, Jen. You deserve it. Plus,"—and here's the only part I really heard—"these floors look so tacky now."

Tacky? Did I hear that right?

Are my floors really so tacky?

As the evening continued, my eyes kept gravitating toward those "tacky" floors. Those tacky floors that had welcomed guests from cities and countries around the world. Those tacky floors that invited children to wrestle and giggle and build forts on top of them. Those tacky floors where thousands of feet had walked during hundreds of gatherings. Those tacky floors that had both celebrated new life and supported the hearts of mourners. Those tacky floors that had witnessed so much grace in action, all while refusing to disclose the secrets they heard. Those tacky floors that told stories of a life well spent. Could any model home really replace what I loved so much about these tacky floors?

A few days after that party, I received word that the new flooring project had been put on an indefinite hold. This led to several times throughout the next year when our ten-year-old daughter would continue to ask, "Do you think we'll replace our floors soon?"

"I'm not sure, honey, but our floors are just fine."

"No, Mom, they're tacky. You know they are."

Having heard her assessment at least one time too many, I sighed and asked her to come sit with me on the sofa.

"Do you see that stain? Remember when Lola got into the chocolate? And we thought she might die? But she didn't? The Lord took care of your special puppy, and that stain reminds us of that.

"And the places that are torn in the kitchen vinyl? You crawled for the first time over that spot. You took your first steps right by that crack there. And now you're ten years old, dropping cookie dough you made from scratch all by yourself on that same tacky floor.

"See this coffee spot? I smile every time I see it because it reminds me of the night it got there, a really special evening when Aunt Rachel and Aunt Martha, Mrs. Cowen, and I were crying and giggling together, assuring one another we could make it through our exhausting days.

"Sweetie," I pushed on, drawing her in closer to me, "I know you don't like these floors, and it's okay to think about buying new ones. I think about it too, but for now, I want you to love them and all they symbolize. They stand for LIFE. Life to the fullest."

Even as we sat there cuddling together and reminiscing, I could feel the contentment covering us. Yes, worn carpets still stared back at us. Yes, the rips in the flooring couldn't go undetected. But they were ours. Our home, our memories, flowing from God's abundance, our reminder of God's faithfulness throughout a decade of uncertainty.

And thinking now of this moment with my daughter reminds me of that subtle one-word perspective shift you and I talked about: We never *have* to celebrate tacky floors; we *get* to. Yes, they're messy, just like we are. But there's something awfully beautiful in that.

I don't know what your current life circumstances are like as you read this chapter. Perhaps, you're going through a financially challenging season, like we did. And if so—if that's what is forefront in your mind right now—I understand the temptation you may feel to run away and retreat. The thought of vulnerably inviting others into your pain, into a spirit that feels so crushed, is overwhelming.

But I guarantee, during these most difficult times we need one another more than ever. We aren't meant to do life alone. We are meant to share our story with someone else. And we can't let our circumstances keep us separated from the community we need. This may be the time God is asking you to reach out to someone else as she wanders the same road, and together you can encourage each other to stay in the right lane.

So let's come back to the elephant in the room. I won't sugarcoat it: hospitality is easier with money. Having been on both sides, I know. It's easier not having to scour the sales. It's easier not needing to stress about feeding guests on a tight budget. It's easier being able to freely purchase full-price decorative items to spruce up the house. Hosting anything—reality check—not just hosting, *everything in life* is easier with money.

But this is equally true: there was never a sweeter season of sharing our home, our gifts, our time, or the meager offerings we could give than during those years when we were flat broke. Never was I more convinced that circumstances did not determine my peace. The world could neither give me peace nor take it away. I had a choice of what I would cling to. And open-door hospitality helped me cling to Jesus. Our source. Our living water. Only in Him can true peace and plenty be found.

And if I didn't know it then, I got to learn it again.

Yes, a decade after receiving those bags of groceries and other gifts, we entered our second period of unemployment. Again, life was hard. With five kids by then and our eldest sons in high school, the financial crunch was much more real to them this time around. But I'd learned from our earlier life lessons that any wisdom and spiritual growth I experienced had always come as a result of adversity. So I decided again to keep our door open to opportunity.

One way I did it was by chronicling our season of unemployment on my blog. Despite the overwhelming pressure that was weighing on my soul, I knew my only hope was in Christ and in making sure God was glorified by what He was doing in our lives during that time. This seemed like a highly transparent, highly visible, although scary way to do it.

But over the year, as I opened my virtual door, hundreds of thousands of women journeyed with me as I shared practical tips and ideas for living on less—everything from frugal recipes, pantry challenges, and do-it-yourself home décor inspiration, to frugal fashionista finds and other ways to slash an unslashable budget. My little corner on the Internet served as a launching place for women everywhere to encourage one another on the journey.

I was stunned by the response. I'd been willing to go first, sharing our mess, and it ultimately became my message. Because when we link arms together in our sisterhood of the imperfect, we can always be sure women will gather.

In fact, as more and more women began dialoguing in the blog comments, I sensed in them a desire for some in-person encouragement. This inspired me to launch the Becoming Conference, with a mission for uniting women together in being creative, frugal, and purposeful. A friend and I invited hundreds of women to join us in learning to be more intentional about all things heart and home. I hauled our family room furniture across the state to decorate the stage, announcing that since they couldn't all come over to sip coffee in my home, I'd brought my family room to *them*. I'm still waiting, planning, and saving for my long-standing dream of building a large barn on our homestead to hold weekends of encouragement for women, but that vision is going to require a lot more than a coupon.

Even that unexpected $100 cashier's check we'd received years before inspired me to design a workshop entitled the "$100 Life," in which I navigate finances and share a creative challenge to revolutionize our homes, hospitality, and even wardrobes by strategically applying $100 to varying aspects of our life. Is it possible to really host and feed a beautiful gathering of fifty people on a $100 budget? Yep, it can be done.

I love God's sense of creativity. I prayed with bold expectation that He would not allow my moments of pain to return void, and He didn't. Those tough periods of time were in no way a waste, not since we'd kept trusting Jesus with our lack and kept our home a transparent place for

Him to work inside. Now I get to use my years of fun thrift store finds, spray-painting escapades, and learning the difference between a need and a want to share the gospel. As I high-five women who hug me and share their latest frugal find or tell me about the credit card debt they're chipping away, I in turn tell them about the One who paid the greatest of debts.

What a story I get to tell. The greatest of them all.

So what did our grannies tell us about polite conversation? About age and weight and the money we make? If you're talking to me, ignore them. I'm an open book. And by the way, I finally got my new floors. I'd love to have you come over sometime and see them yourself.

Just Open the Door

Dear Jen

We are in a season of financial difficulty, and while I want to host, I'm nervous about hosting well on a budget.

Need Help

Dear NH,

Remember, small is the new big; and stress-free, meaningful hospitality is our mantra. It takes creativity, but you still have so many options when hosting on a budget. Most of my budget stems from the food, so don't shoulder the entire meal burden on your own. Friends want to bring something, so make it a potluck.

When I hosted our first spontaneous "After Christmas" open house, everyone brought something, and I served spiral honey ham that was marked down after Christmas for only $5.00. (Same occurs after Easter.) For the cake, I chopped up discounted chocolate Santas (sorry Santa) in place of full-price baking chocolate.

So start from that mind-set. Search the marked-down produce and meat sections at the grocery store. Always buy ahead and focus on sale items, and then adjust your menu plan accordingly. While other people stock up on Black Friday deals, I buy fresh turkeys. Yep, grocery stores are in a frenzy to sell their extras, so I swoop in to feed our family for pennies on the dollar.

Leftovers from my after-Christmas hams stretched into multiple meals: potato ham chowder; ham, cheese, and egg breakfast casserole; grilled tomato, ham, and cheese sandwiches; navy beans and split pea soup using the ham hock. Four meals for seven people totaled $20.00 with fruit and vegetables. You can do this!

Jen

134

Elevate the Ordinary

❁ Creating a cozy home ambiance doesn't require a big budget. There are so many creative ways to add a fresh touch without breaking the bank.

❁ Paint: Whether it's repainting walls (find mismatched paint for $5.00 at home improvement stores) or freshening an old piece of furniture, paint packs the biggest punch for your dollar.

❁ Shop your own home and yard. Place flowers or plants in Mason jars, wooden bowls, glass bottles, vases, pots, or any other unique object you find.

❁ Find mismatched glassware and serving pieces of similar color. If it's a party theme, one of my go-tos is to spray-paint decorative accent pieces and candlesticks to match my colors.

❁ Cake pedestals and trays are favorites for decorating because they're both stylish and functional, and you can find them for a few dollars. Group and layer decorative or similar food items together on the tray or pedestal for an organized, clean look. When you need to clear space on the table, you can simply remove the entire tray. It couldn't be easier to ready your table for use.

❁ Twinkly lights: No matter the month, string white lights. Everything is always better with a little sparkle.

12

A Home That
Says "Welcome"

I don't know if anyone's ever fully prepared for the delicate and trying balancing act of launching our children into adulthood. As moms, we spend the first eighteen years of our kids' lives bouncing between daily, mundane mothering tasks and attempting to lay for them a solid spiritual, emotional, and social foundation. Then in the largest feat of parental surrender, we step back, release control, and give them the necessary space to spread their wings . . . solo.

When our firstborn, our truth teller, was nearing that stage himself, he repeatedly let it be known he couldn't wait to be out of our house and on his own. So I gave him a lot of space. But not too many weeks after we'd dropped him off at college many hours from home, the phone calls started coming. Each one more often. Each one more honest.

"Mom, I just want to come home," he finally came out and said. What, did he need money already? Was he not getting along with his roommate? Was he being the protective big brother checking in on his little sisters?

No, that wasn't it, or at least not all of it. But as the calls continued, it hit me. He wanted to hear our voices. He ached for a piece of home. And in our last phone conversation before he came home for fall break, even more of it came out. His words revealed a raw and rare vulnerability, one I hadn't expected from our extremely-confident-on-the-surface, can-always-do-it-alone guy.

"Mom, I need to tell you something." His voice cracked a little as he paused to gather his thoughts. "I know I was super cocky about this whole transition thing. I didn't think I'd have a difficult adjustment, and I never thought I'd struggle with homesickness at all. But it's been a challenging semester. And I just want you to know, I can't wait to get home. My soul needs it, and I'm so excited to be with you guys."

Ahhh. (Thank you.)

I'll never forget that call. Summed up in a few short sentences was a gift every parent desires. This moment marked so much more than a child eagerly anticipating a home-cooked meal. It marked a heart softening to the Holy Spirit and years of answered prayer for my husband and me, standing in the gap on behalf of our children. Even with an imperfect home filled with sinful parents and siblings, unmade beds, cluttered closets, and leftovers in the fridge, he knew our home represented a refuge, a spiritual center, a place to belong. He knew it reflected a tiny glimmer of God's character, a place that symbolizes welcome, where life is renewed, hope is restored, and a feast of life awaits. It took his being separated from everything he'd ever known to fully appreciate the welcoming hospitality of it, but our son—bless his heart, as we say in the South—just wanted to come home! My momma's heart explodes when I swing open the doors with a "Welcome home" to our precious children.

There's something incredibly unique about the concept of home. We know it's not about the building or structure. It's bigger than that. No matter our past wounds, no matter our poor decisions, no matter our previous family history, a longing is knitted into every single one of us to find a place to call home. This is not something earmarked for believers alone; it's a common denominator that everyone senses, even if they struggle to put a name on it—which is why, as people saved by grace, we want to create an atmosphere that says "welcome" to all. Pointing others toward home is truly the heart of our most important ministry.

But . . .

The best invitation we can ever offer to anyone is to those who share our lives on a daily basis, the loved ones right in our home and family. That's where the truest form of hospitality begins. Our spouse and kids, those we do life with day-to-day, are our closest neighbors, and our priority must begin with them before we think of extending ministry to others. Our hearts are made for home. And we must make it a safe landing place where our children will always want to return. And be welcomed.

But in addition to being our children's landing place, home is also their learning lab. Just as we bear responsibility to create a welcoming environment for *them,* we also need to show them how to grow a welcoming heart toward *others.* This gives us a whole new reason for allowing life-on-life ministry to flow in and out of our homes: it cultivates within our kids a generational legacy of hospitality and service. They learn it by watching; they learn it by doing.

Our sons and daughters, our boys and girls, our teens and college students—the children (or grandchildren) right under our roof—represent the thought leaders of the future in work, ministry, worldview, ethics, and culture. We are training and discipling a new generation of world changers. Yes, it's an overwhelming and nearly paralyzing concept at times, one that can seem far beyond our reach to accomplish. But it's a calling we should receive as the highest privilege given. And I can't think of a better way of doing it—of tangibly exhibiting missional living—than by simply creating a life-giving home that says welcome. As we reshape our preconceived notions about hospitality and align them with God's Word, we create a powerfully interactive life lab for our children. And an exciting new legacy for our family.

Think of it. Through this "welcome home" lens, our children begin to view every person God brings through our doors as divine interventions amid their everyday life. By watching us serve, they learn how to partner with us by living out the Great Commandment and sharing the gospel. As we demonstrate how much we value those different from us, as we affirm others' unique personalities and listen to their stories, our kids learn to do the same. Through hands-on interaction with us, they see what it means to be the hands and feet of Jesus by becoming the church of God in our own home. As we walk alongside them, they're able to imitate us in living a life on purpose.

It's all part of Deuteronomy 6 parenting: "These words that I am giving you today are to be in your heart. Repeat them to your children. Talk about them when you sit in your house and when you walk along the road, when you lie down and when you get up" (vv. 6–7).

It's not easy, no. But as the Lord is quick to remind me, I'm not so easy either.

In fact, let me say—in terms of viewing my home as a learning lab—the lessons start with me. Home may be the heart of my most important ministry, but regrettably it's also the place where my sin bubbles over more often than anywhere else. I fumble through many days begging the Lord that His power would be made perfect in my weakness. Home is where I am the most exposed, the most exhausted, where my family sees the good, the bad, and everything in between.

But because of this, it's also where the transformative power of Christ can best be seen in me. It's the place where He's most likely to begin chiseling away at my sinful heart, drawing me closer to Him and showering me with His sufficient grace. And just as serving others in Jesus' name proves to be the antidote for my own self-centeredness, it works in my children's hearts as well. Just as living a life of welcome roots me, shifts my focus toward others, and stops my wandering heart, it does the same for them.

Living a life of welcome lets us cast a long-term, multigenerational vision for our children. By being part of a welcoming home, they learn tangible life skills that allow hospitality to become a natural outflow of their lives, regardless of their gifting or personalities. They're being equipped day by day to enter the future knowing how to build community in an age of isolation, how to make memories in a generation mobilized by technology, how to create an environment of discipleship among people yearning for godly mentors.

That's creating legacy. Right here. In the laboratories of our own homes.

I've watched our teen daughter struggle through her science lab this semester. She prepares her hypothesis, an educated guess. Then based on the results, she tweaks her findings by observing what worked and what didn't. The more she experiments, the more she learns and improves in her studies.

Shouldn't our homes be like that too? As we grow in our understanding of hospitality, our homes become the ultimate life lab experiment, where together we learn, tweak, experiment, and grow, getting better at what we do while getting our kids ready for a life of fruitful, kingdom-focused endeavors.

I've brainstormed a broad number of ways our various roles, needs, and identities provide us with opportunities for growth and investment as a family. This list is by no means exhaustive, but hopefully it's long enough to inspire you with a few of the training grounds that show up organically when you embrace an open-door, welcoming lifestyle together.

Opportunities for Growth and Investment

As Parents

When we invite others into our homes, we receive a deeper insight into our children's character by observing how they interact with guests of varying ages. It gives us the chance to identify areas where they need guidance.

One of our daughters, for instance, is by nature a quieter, shyer, more introverted child. Some parents excuse their introverted children from conversations with guests, but I think this does them a disservice. By viewing hospitality as a learning lab, you can help your kids overcome their shyness by practicing communication skills from the comfort of your own home.

With our daughter, we didn't push nerve-racking conversations; we simply expected and encouraged direct eye contact with small, baby-step interactions. She is now one of our best hosts, understands how to graciously welcome, makes delightful introductions, and is one of our best listeners. Introverts often have an amazing gift of hospitality toward small groups or one-on-one interactions, and as parents we can call this gifting up from within them by giving them patient, persistent practice.

As Hosts

Hosting others consistently calls us to move past our nervousness and hesitance, choosing to believe that how we love and serve our neighbor impacts the kingdom. As we step forward in obedience, risking insecurity and uncertainty, we show our children (and others) what it looks like to walk outside our comfort zone. Freedom and delight often result from taking that risky step.

In addition, it helps us train our children in basic life skills. Anytime we open our home, for example, good food is always involved. Our kids have learned that food doesn't have to be fancy, but they can each now make basic snacks, a simple meal, and our famous taco dip without a recipe. Even as our two oldest sons have moved into an apartment, they send me pictures of their groceries, how much they have saved, and what they've made. We also insist when hosting that the bathrooms are spotless; other areas, merely presentable. As a result, our kids know how to shape up our main living areas quickly (I admit, relocating miscellaneous clutter into a plastic bin and hiding it works wonders), and they've mastered the simple cleaning tasks of a home.

As Tired Women

Sometimes opening our home is the last thing we desire to do, but doing so anyway out of obedience gives us an opportunity to talk it through with our kids. I don't communicate it with a complaining spirit (well, most of the time, anyhow), but simply tell them, "I'm exhausted. I don't really know these people, and honestly, I don't feel like opening my door right now. Let's ask the Lord for extra strength that we can give away and make this a special evening for all of us." It's healthy to discuss our reservations and areas of struggle with them because sometimes it's truly a labor of love. When they witness how you give your worries, your exhaustion, or frustrations to the Lord, your vulnerability opens future doors of authentic communication.

It also gives them (and us) opportunities for learning to choose gratitude over complaining. Again, the Bible says to "offer hospitality to one another without grumbling" (1 Pet. 4:9 NIV). "Grumbling," in terms of practicing hospitality, often means making excuses. "I don't have extra money in the budget. My kids are too young, my house is a mess, and our schedule is crazy." We need to model gratitude over complaining.

As Hurting People

I went through a season of refusing to do the inviting. But let my daughter's following statement to me be a lesson to all of us that pretending everything is fine doesn't fool our kids. "Mom," she said, "we're not having people over anymore, and I really miss it." Her disappointment became my wake-up call.

"Emma, you're right," I said, "I've been allowing my pity party and feelings to get in the way. I'm so glad Jesus hasn't stopped reaching out to me. Let's pick a day right now when we can extend an invitation." Isolation and loneliness are two of the most strategic tools Satan uses. I repented and begged the Lord to shift my "woe is me" attitude to elevate JOY (Jesus, Others, You) to its rightful position. Then I asked my daughter's forgiveness and recommitted to sharing this gift of invitation that changes everything.

But we do well to be honest with one another that, yes, sometimes all of us hurt. And just as we need others to notice and care for us through our low times, we should be watching for how to lift the burdens others carry, developing a spirit of empathy, compassion, and gentleness. Our teens, for example, sensitive to giving young mommas a respite who are visiting our home, have learned to pop babies on their hip and soothe them. If another child looks sad or lonely, we encourage our children to come alongside them and invite them into their circle.

All of this helps our children start early practicing the ministry of awareness by looking for those who are alone or left out. Sometimes they'll get rejected, sure, but their responsibility is to do the inviting and leave the results to God. Some children will always be better at this than others, but we can still point them to do the right thing. An open home gives them that chance.

As Leaders

Living a legacy of hospitality isn't a one-and-done occurrence. Over time it allows us to model—be it ever so imperfectly—how to lead and serve with flexibility as we live life in front of our guests and children.

They observe, for example, how my husband loves me, honors me, and, yes, even has fun teasing me. They view how we may disagree but then how we commit ourselves to resolving issues in a healthy manner. While sometimes it's critical to do this behind closed doors, the nature of home life is such that we often work through certain issues in an open-air context, which hopefully shows a biblical model of confrontation and resolution.

Guests sense how we deal with disciplinary issues, which often leads to dinnertime dialogue about the necessity of parental consistency. As we mess up (more than we like), they watch us extend grace and seek to own our mistakes. Young couples have shared that observing seasoned parents in action has helped them create a plan of action for their own family.

Leading also involves demonstrating a boldness for Christ and His Word. By letting our kids see us praying out loud in front of others and giving words of blessing and encouragement to our guests, they've been given the opportunity to do the same.

As Stewards

One of the best ways of demonstrating that all we own belongs to God is when a guest accidentally ruins the dining room table. (Ask me how I know.) They'll see in a hurry what matters most to us. For while we don't discount the care of what He has given us—and trust me, I get up in our boys' business when they break things by roughhousing with friends after I've repeatedly told them to stop—I welcome those noises any day over the silence of stale living.

When hospitality is a way of life, dishes will break, carpets will get stained, foods will spill—and our children will watch with bated breath and take notes on how we respond to the mishaps. Do we spew and react, or do we pause, gather, and then respond sensitively? Are we making known our priorities of elevating people over possessions? Are we living on mission with our motives?

Even on a childhood level, the presence of others in the home helps them learn to share toys and give up prized possessions in order to honor a guest above themselves. It provides ample opportunities to grow in generosity and combats a pervasive entitlement mentality as they make room for one more, even if it's not comfortable.

As Communicators

Hospitality is a communication exercise. We model how to engage deep conversations around the table, how to tap into critical-thinking skills, and how to facilitate higher-level discussions by the continuous art of asking good questions. Nothing is off limits at the table (except phones and bodily noises; I have to routinely squash both of those), and it's always a safe place to give your opinion. Depending on the guests, this may even result in a hefty back-and-forth of vigorous disagreement, but everyone hugs and leaves as friends. Shouldn't we have more of that?

It also trains and teaches the art of listening attentively to others when they're speaking. By not always feeling the need to react and respond, we help our kids understand the power behind someone's story and how to begin to tell their own.

As Respecters of People

Every person who enters our home is, like us, created in the image of God. Therefore, if for no other reason, they deserve to be treated with respect. Having them here gives us an opportunity to learn and teach the importance of displaying good manners.

With repetition, manners become second nature to our kids, but they need lots of reminders when they're young. I didn't want to be a nagging mother, constantly interrupting with others around, so I taught them some basic sign language for things like "please," "thank you," "no, thank you," and eye contact, and I could easily use these reminders without anyone knowing. Yes, even during their teen years, I could send a signal clear across the room, and they'd know exactly what I meant.

But not only does open-home life provide practice of good manners, it also enhances the ability to interact well with diverse groups of people—multicultural, multiracial, singles, widows, and the elderly, to name a few. Recently one of the single, German employees at my husband's work mentioned, "Your daughter was the first to show me what a s'more was. I could barely speak any English and had only been in the States for a few weeks, but she sat with me around the bonfire at your house and walked me through my first s'more. I'll always remember that." What a tangible reminder that sometimes love is best shown by unwrapping a chocolate bar together.

See what I mean? Opportunities for growth and coaching abound. And by looking for them, by taking advantage of them, you'll know you are investing skills in young hearts that will play out into their own lives and will then multiply across the generations.

None of these things happen overnight. And none of us run the learning lab perfectly. But in giving our children repeated exposure to others through the open doors of our lives, some of these qualities can't help but happen over time. Practicing hospitality is an ongoing process that is always worth it. Who knows where it will take you and your children next?

It's sure to be a welcome place when you get there.

We've sent three children off to college now, and many times throughout the school year we've received the same call as we did with our oldest: "I can't wait to come home, Mom." But because the Lord led us to create a home full of joy and laughter, where life is celebrated in abundance, we often hear them adding this tag-on: "My friends all want to come home with me, too. They can't wait either."

You think they're welcome here? Absolutely!

Swing wide the door so others can flourish. Encourage them, laugh with them, welcome them just as they are because when your home produces the walking, talking, open door, open fridge, comfy sofa invitation into the presence of Christ, people will be drawn to it. And when your children grow up in a home marked by hospitality and blessing, it becomes an overflow of who they are as well. They can't help but embrace the gift of invitation and pass on His love to others.

Oh friend, it's all because our hearts were made for home.

Dear Jen

We have a guest room, and I'd love to designate it as an open door for anyone who wants to use it. I'm starting with a weekend visit from my mother-in-law. I'm anxious, though, because she normally stays in a hotel and she'll need a place to escape the chaos. What thoughtful touches make your guest room extra comfy?

The Daughter-in-Law

Dear Daughter-in-Law,

I love that you care enough to create an atmosphere that is welcoming. We're all starting somewhere, and creating a cozy, inviting space is a great beginning. A few thoughts:

- Sound machine or fan
- Extra pillows and blanket
- Fresh flowers on the nightstand
- Welcome note on the pillow with a few mints, chocolates, and magazines
- Framed picture of her with your family
- Basket of toiletries: hair dryer, extra washcloths, toothbrush and toothpaste, heating pad
- Flashlight or nightlight
- Instructions on how to use the remote control (print out a picture of it, and write the steps on it)
- Favorite movies (ask ahead for ones she'd like to see, and leave them by the TV)

Jen

Elevate the Ordinary

❀ Traditions are the "we always" of family heritage.[14] Invest time into cultivating a strong sense of identity by establishing meaningful traditions throughout the year (not just the holidays). "We always" go to the mountains as an extended family to cut down our Christmas tree. "We always" serve breakfast in bed on our special tray for birthdays. "We always" have family devotions on the beach at 11:00 a.m. during our family vacation. These anticipated traditions create strong family ties that will keep your children wanting to come home.

❀ Mark rite-of-passage, memory-making moments with meaningful times of verbal and written blessings alongside much celebration. We mark key ages like thirteen, sixteen, and high school graduation, plus baby showers, marriage, and milestone anniversaries.

❀ Create a home where your children want to hang out. Laugh often, be silly for no reason, and celebrate simple moments with abandon. Embarrass your kids in the happiest way possible at least once a month. Be a "yes" mom as often as you can, so that your carefully chosen no's are received without a battle (although you'll still have those).

❀ Create a family text group on your phones. It's one of my favorite things, and we text nearly every day. We post funny pictures, jokes, updates on football and "love interests" or lack thereof (ha), as well as prayer requests, encouragement, and cheering one another on. It keeps us connected and involved in one another's lives even when we're away from home.

EXTRA HELPING *from my dad (Dick Van Eerden)*

A Legacy of Welcome

Everybody leaves a legacy of some kind—great, good, indifferent, or bad!

A father who loves his wife well is continually blessing his children with a legacy. And think about the multigenerational effect that can occur when a dad trains up and gifts his children with wisdom regarding biblical principles of money and finance, while also making choices that result in a godly inheritance for his grandchildren.

Parents can reasonably expect the same kind of old-age treatment that grandparents have received from them. Kids (and grandkids) are *always* watching, learning, cataloging (good or bad)—and these thousands of impressions are the guts of what legacy building is really all about. What we do always speaks so much louder than what we say.

When my wife and I were in our early thirties, we decided to accept and serve the Lord (Josh. 24:15) and to become a first-generation Christian family. Until then we'd been on track to leave a legacy of indifference. Then, several years later, Ruth Bell Graham (Billy Graham's wife) encouraged my bride at a conference, "You could start your own Christian heritage . . . right now . . . no matter what the details were of your previous background." This led to the real genesis moment of the intentionality phase of our legacy building. Together, we purposefully labored, for many hours, to carefully craft our simple but focused Personal Life Purpose Statement:

> To support others in discovering the truth so that their expectations will be realized, their lives will be enhanced, and both of us will experience the peace that comes from obedience to God.

Our Life Purpose Statement has been functional for us, and it has been cured with aging. Initially, every word was examined, valued, dissected, filtered again, tweaked, and retested. This process continued until my bride and I were in complete harmony with its expected effect on our future actions, commitments, and relationships. It is outward and upward focused, and it both restrains and energizes our response to all incoming challenges and opportunities.

Bottom line: it has worked for us.

The "open door" component of our family legacy certainly correlates, in large measure, to the oversized servant's heart of my bride. We've always had great food at our open family table, an open guest bed, and thousands of hours of both surface and deep, life-changing conversations.

These times were always in the bull's-eye zone of our Personal Life Purpose Statement. Our open door has resulted in building precious lifetime relationships among our guest registry of more than sixty international students we have hosted, countless missionaries, single and pregnant moms, recovering addicts, foster babies, runaway teens, touring groups, visiting athletes, starry-eyed engaged love birds, and married couples in crisis.

From our current perspective in life, it's amazing and gratifying for my wife and me to see a similar open door in the homes of our children.

While we've failed in many areas and would love do-overs, we've been blessed beyond our fair measure. Being intentional with our family's purpose has led to incredible opportunities for hospitality, growth, and blessing. And we wouldn't want it any other way. That's our legacy for now. Stand by as we covenant to finish strong . . . together.

13

If Teacups and Coffee Cups Could Talk

While spontaneous, stress-free, and nearly always imperfect hospitality works best with my busy lifestyle, there's something pretty spectacular about slowing down and creating meaningful beauty for our guests when the opportunity arises.

At some time, all of us have dreamed about that magical Cinderella moment, and admittedly I am a fairy godmother wannabe. I want to make those dreams come true, and every once in a while, I do.

One day, for a special pair of guests (whom I'll introduce to you in a moment), I decided to pull out all the stops and set an elegant table. I knew it had been an exhausting week for them, so I'd chosen this extra gesture as a way of honoring them, blessing them, and reminding them how much they're valued and worthy of celebrating. So I placed two long, silver tapers in crystal candleholders on the table and arranged freshly cut roses so they spilled from the intricately hand-painted vase situated in the center. Delicate, English teacups and saucers waited patiently, while their accompanying sterling silver spoons sat on starched cloth napkins.

As soft, classical music played sweetly in the background, I took time to rest my soul. I inhaled the sweet smell of the flowers and stared into the twinkling tea lights scattered around the lace tablecloth. Leisurely, I took my time arranging the lovely tea tray, even as I felt the earlier morning's chaos begin to slip away. I could sense an unexpected pleasure arising in my heart from this change of pace, and I enjoyed focusing on the creative, little details I normally rush through. With the sugar bowl and cream pitcher filled, I even sprinkled a few rose petals around the tray.

Perfect.

Then I began to warm the china teapot, remembering the day I'd discovered it nestled in a quaint English antique store during my semester abroad as a young college student. The shopkeeper's passion assured me that the one tiny chip on its bottom was purely cosmetic in nature, so I felt affirmed in rescuing it at a price I could afford. With the excitement and kinship I felt for this lonely piece no one else wanted, I wrapped it up tight and hand-carried it through ten different airports in five countries. Oh, the stories it could tell. I still wonder how many hands, like mine, have meticulously filled it throughout its century or more of use. Had those tea servers ever been as eager as I am to hear the stories this old teapot might tell once poured out among the table?

The doorbell snapped me from my reminiscing, and I hurried to greet my long-anticipated guests. To call these sweet ladies kindred spirits would be more true of them than anyone else in the world to me. *My daughters.* They stood there smiling in their floral skirts and white gloves, with precious pearls cascading down the front of their beautiful attire.

"Madams," I said as I opened the door, welcoming them with the best British accent I could muster. "I'm so thrilled you've accepted my invitation. Won't you please follow me? Our afternoon together awaits, and I assure you, it will be simply marvelous."

"Momma, aren't you supposed to kiss our hands?" they inquired with their arms outstretched, daintily bent at the wrist. I stifled my laughter at the black Nike swoosh symbols that subtly appeared from underneath their long sleeves, betraying their "tea-ready" wardrobe accessory as actually being their brother's white golf gloves. Having kissed their hands, I leaned my forehead against theirs, and one daughter at a time I whispered, "Do you know how special you are?"

"Yes, Momma."

"Why are you special?"

"Because God made me special."

"That's right. You are God's precious princess, and there is no other Abigail Lynn or Emma Angelee Schmidt in the whole world. He made you unique, adored, and I still can't believe I get to be your mommy."

Since they often hear me saying this, I always dramatize this most important part: "I can hardly believe that out of all the girls in the whole world, He picked little ol' me to be your mommy. I still can't even believe it! Me!"

"Yes, Mom, we know," they giggled as they rolled their eyes. "You and Dad tell us this *all the time*."

"We just never want you to forget how much we love you."

"Now," I pronounced, resuming my best British impression, "let's get on with our tea party, shall we?"

I carried the freshly spray-painted tray to our foyer, where I'd placed the converted card table by our front door expressly for this special occasion. Stretched across it was the beautifully embroidered tablecloth I'd once purchased at Goodwill—another item which reminds me of its own remarkable story every time I grab it from my linen closet. I'm always grateful for the unknown maker's talent and her time-consuming handiwork.

Before the girls sat down, I let them pick out any teacup from my collection. Each cup (you guessed it) has a unique story as well, and often the girls want to hear it told again. From local antique stores to international travels, inherited or given as gifts, I've tried to mark each one with a date and a place to trigger my memories.

As I poured lemonade into their distinctive teacups, I prayed their hearts would be sweetened with His goodness and their souls filled to the brim with His everlasting love and kindness. Piling their etched-glass plates high with Doritos (yes, their favorite), I affirmed the special and unique roles they played in the kingdom of God. I knew my girls didn't understand those sentiments yet, but I trusted—and continue to trust—that as I practice the presence of slowing down and fostering meaningful moments like these with them, my nurturing of beauty within their souls will help lay the foundation for truth.

We laughed and giggled, slowly sipped and nibbled, and as our eldest daughter requested more "tea," I soon found her steering the conversation in a surprising fashion, opening up with her sister and me about some of the struggles she was experiencing as a young fourth-grader. Hmm. Curious that she would wait until tea time to so deeply reveal herself. Had I missed picking up on these concerns of hers in our normal routine? Had she simply interpreted this extra time focused on her as an invitation to a more intimate glimpse into her heart?

Not all time is created equal. The leisurely spirit of tea time seems to give permission to drop one's guard. Cozy moments like these feel safe and inviting. They point toward intimate conversation and relationship that is beautiful *for itself*, without any other contributors vying for a share of recognition. It's a time of confirmation where we're made to feel important and loved because that's the only possible explanation for someone wanting to spend it so intentionally with us. Tea time is simply for the sake of learning about and enjoying one another.

So put yourself at that table with us. Can you envision it? Close your eyes for a minute, take a big cleansing sigh, and imagine yourself pulling up a seat. Wouldn't you love a few hours of similar refreshment? What would *you* feel like you could share with someone in that kind of setting?

The guests at my tea parties have changed throughout the years, but sharing a cup of kindness spans generations. When we prioritize time to fill someone's cup, it becomes a gateway to fill her heart and soul with the things that matter most. We hope to settle her unsettled spirit and see her leave with her cup overflowing.

It doesn't have to be anything fancy or elaborate, although I do love an excuse to set a beautiful table-scape. I've been known to mimic my Princess Diana girl-crush days with linens and silver, flowers and scones. But it's definitely not about perfecting an Earl Grey blend, since I'm 100 percent a coffee girl myself. There's just something innately life-giving about allowing a semblance of serenity to interrupt our frenzied day through the art of tea time (or coffee or hot chocolate).

To stop. To sit. To still our hearts.

Taking tea together reminds us to mimic Jesus' pace. He was never too busy. He was never in a hurry. *Frantic* was not a part of His vocabulary. He lingered. Jesus demonstrated stillness as one of the leading requirements for learning the Father's heart. "Be still" is not solely a rebuke to our antsy kids; it's a real address reminding God's children that we must eliminate unnecessary distraction and haste from our lives in order to know God intimately.

Sometimes this Christlike attitude of calmness requires some serious faith—a faith that says, "Lord, You know all that's on my plate this week. Would You bless my decision to set aside some time to rest and be intentional with those around me?" At other times, what may be necessary is not so much a deeper trust that God will provide the means of completing everything on the to-do list but rather a heart that genuinely delights in the simple pleasures and truly yearns for the nearness that's brewed among teacups late into the evening.

We sit. We rest. We take intentional moments with Him.

Tea affords us this time.

My first introduction to the art of taking afternoon tea began right after I graduated from high school. I spent one semester attending a Bible school in England, as I mentioned, where they still embraced this longstanding ritual.

Every afternoon, I'd eye the clock impatiently, waiting for my favorite sound of the day: the ringing bell signifying our tea break. All activities stopped during that hour, and we gathered together in community over our choice of hot beverages. While waiting for the tea to cool, we'd huddle into groups, sharing prayer requests or otherwise erupting in laughter. The art of taking tea was a tool—an avenue—to prioritize people over productivity. As a nineteen-year-old girl, I witnessed how those simple moments of gathering together spoke into the depths of our souls.

When I returned to the States, embracing this time-honored tradition began to revolutionize many aspects of my concept of hospitality. I started a collection of all things "high tea." *Downton Abbey* wasn't even a thought at the time, but I understand the draw of its pageantry. I bought teacups and teapots, silver pieces, and special linens. I'd pick up mismatched crystal goblets at yard sales and do a happy dance in our van whenever I found treasured silver trays for a few dollars. It wasn't out of the ordinary for me to serve our kids their frozen pizza on china by candlelight. When the kids ran in from playing outside and asked for a glass of water, they didn't blink if I handed it to them in fluted glassware. Why do we wait and only do those things for company?

When friends stopped by, I wanted them to feel pampered. It might take me an extra minute to light a few candles, pour hot coffee in a china teacup, and gather a glass tray to spread out some fresh baked goodies (straight from the grocer shelves). But again, must all our coffee come from the drive-through window? Must all our tea come from swirling a package of instant powder?

A good cup of tea, like the perfect cup of coffee, can't be rushed without circumventing its original intent. Whether we soothe our souls by candlelight or cuddle up on the front porch, carving out small moments of meaningful beauty can touch a place deep within us. When we elevate that moment to include another person, it exemplifies the true loveliness of gathering for tea. It gives us permission to slow down and be intentional with the gift of someone's time.

So I recommend to you this form of hospitality that is so soothing in its simplicity: the beauty of a shared cup of kindness.

In our culture where shortcuts, quick fixes, and instant anything are the beverage of choice, I choose to invest in a slow nurturing of the senses. While boiling water on the stove and waiting for the kettle to whistle, we create space to be fully present without distraction. In those first moments as the teabags steep, we can light a candle and begin to unwind. Sharing a cup of kindness is a simple ritual that takes time. The magic occurs in the preparation and enjoyment of it. When we attempt to rush the process, we miss out on the best parts—the tranquility and delight that stem from the simple pleasures of life.

I'm sure you've caught the irony by now that even after I fell in love with the idea of teatime and began practicing the spirit of it with family and guests, I never did fall in love with the taste of tea itself. I know, I know—I tried, I really did. But not preferring the taste of tea hasn't stopped me from applying the same principle of slow appreciation.

I buy whole coffee beans and grind them fresh every morning. I anticipate my coffee as the brewer percolates, though sometimes in my impatience I pour a cup before it's finished, wiping up the drips behind me. I light a candle, grab my Bible, snuggle up in my favorite chair, and ask the Lord to show me what He has for me today while I inhale the best smell I know. It warms my heart to sit next to my daughters as they brew their hot tea. I've passed on the love of it, even if my teacup (or my clunky ceramic mug) holds coffee instead. Yet for both, the premise is still the same—create a gracious atmosphere that feeds the soul and allows for unhurried conversation and refreshment.

One spring afternoon, a friend stopped by for only an hour. Just like tea, friendships take time, and she was determined to squeeze in the small amount of availability she did have. Our kids ran rambunctiously in and out of the house, spilled chips, and turned sticks from the yard into pretend swords, while her toddler tried to ride our yellow lab. Yet there we were: two friends sharing life together, unfazed by the chaos.

As the kids got louder, we moved closer. With candles burning, hot tea steeping, and soft music playing in the background (not that we could hear it), my kitchen table transformed into a place of unhurried refuge where hearts connected. We laughed, pretended we didn't see the kids jumping off the sofa, and allowed our hearts to soak up these small, uninterrupted moments.

When she'd first arrived, I was exhausted, but soon my weariness had disappeared. An afternoon that started with two overwhelmed mommas gave way to a small respite from our typical day. Our bodies and souls were rejuvenated, not by sitting in solitude (although we would have welcomed that too) but through the company and conversation of a dear friend.

While most elegant tea parties are those that are planned well in advance, with beautifully handwritten invitations and lavish teas, keep alert and mindful of those spontaneous moments when your cup of kindness offered to a weary friend may be her answered prayer. This life-giving, sacred spirit of teatime brings beauty and encouragement to everyone.

If only my teacups and coffee mugs could talk, oh, the stories they'd tell.

Dear Jen

I've always loved to throw large dinner parties. I spend months planning, but my favorite part is making every detail look special and elegant. I'm finding it hard not to make it an "entertaining" event.

Trying to Balance the Struggle

Dear Balancing,

The fact that you noticed the struggle means you're exactly where God wants you. It's common to sense this tension between welcome and worry. God created beauty and artistry; part of us is wired to create. If this is one of your gifts that brings God glory, indulge in it; don't apologize for it. Go all out and give your guests a glimpse of what feasting together in heaven might be someday because God cares about those special touches. Just don't forget to invite me.

But remember, while our efficient lists can bring helpful direction, sometimes they suffocate our joy because we're too caught up in creating the perfect details. I continue to ask myself these heart-check questions as I plan for any guests:

- Why am I doing this?
- What's my motivation?
- Who is receiving the honor?

Our goal should be to create a special place where people are welcomed into community and can encounter Jesus more fully. Jesus showed His appreciation for Martha's hard work (Luke 10:38–42), but He wanted to direct her focus on the best thing: the ministry of presence. She practiced limited hospitality. Her heart started in the right place, but she didn't take time to engage once she organized the tasks at hand—and that's what we want to avoid.

While I share many informal stories, there's something magical about taking the paper plates up a notch, creating a fabulous tablescape and throwing a lavish dinner party. Every once in a while, I do the same because I know that at Christ's final feast, every detail will be magnificent.

Jen

ulelees

Elevate the Ordinary

❀ Creating a safe environment for conversation always seems better when we turn off the lights and eat dinner by candlelight, even if it's frozen pizza. This is our daily dinner tradition. You wouldn't believe the number of teenage boys who've mentioned how they think it's the coolest thing ever and who tell me to let their mom know she should burn her candles.

❀ Keep a store-bought, frozen pound cake (or frozen cookie dough) in your freezer at all times. Because with a few quick and easy dessert ideas in your repertoire, you can have a beautifully festive table ready in minutes. Here are four doctored pound cake ideas using store-bought cake. I can attest they pair perfectly with both coffee and tea.

1. Turtle Pound Cake

Cut the pound cake into cubes and place them in dessert dishes. (I love having glass dishes on hand because they dress up any dessert. These are easily found at yard sales or thrift stores for anywhere from twenty-five to seventy-five cents, or visit your local dollar store.) Drizzle the pound cakes with chocolate ice cream topping or hot fudge and caramel topping. Top with pecans and a dab of whipped cream.

2. Stuffed Strawberry Pound Cake

Slice the thawed pound cake horizontally in half. Spread soft (or whipped) cream cheese on the bottom layer, and then top with strawberry preserves (or your favorite preference). Replace the top cake layer, and then top with additional cream cheese and melted preserves. Since I love my cream cheese a bit sweeter, I mix in a bit of sugar to sweeten it, or you could use strawberry cream cheese as well. Serve with whip cream and berries. Fresh is the best, but in winter I substitute frozen berries, and it's still delicious.

3. Lemon or Raspberry Pound Cake

Slice cake horizontally into three layers. Spread lemon curd or raspberry jam between layers, and serve with a dab of whipped cream. Top with cute, curled lemon peel, if desired.

4. Drizzled Pound Cake

Use a fork to poke holes into the top of the thawed pound cake. Drizzle your favorite flavored coffee syrup or cooking liqueur over the cake. Serve immediately, or cover and chill. Before serving, garnish with your favorite fruit, and serve with lots of yummy whipped cream.

(If all else fails: cut, slice, and dunk in coffee. My favorite.)

14

Spontaneous vs. On Purpose

Which statement would you say is the most accurate?
A. Hospitality is best when it's spontaneous.
B. Hospitality is best when it's done on purpose.
I say the answer is easy. It's yes!

Some of the most beautiful, meaningful, hilarious, unforgettable, bonding, faith-building times of my life have come equally from both spontaneous gatherings and those hosted with a specific purpose in mind.

So in this highly practical chapter that I hope you'll bookmark and underline and transfer from book page to daily planner, I want to flood you with ideas and stories you can personalize to your own life. I don't know about you, but I love hearing others' creative ideas.

Having an open door means you're open to anything. So if you're more of an A (carefree and laid back), or you're more of a B (appreciate an intentional plan), consider opening your heart and mind to how the other half lives, letting God round you into someone He can easily position wherever He needs you to be, loving on whomever He needs you to love.

Spontaneous versus On Purpose: it's beautiful any way you look at it.

I finished leading the last worship song, and it just kind of came out: "I know it's last-minute, but after the service today, I'd love to invite you all over for lunch. I have some chili on the stove, but if you can pick up something to share on the way, that would be great."

Newly married, bright-eyed, and filled with a passion to influence my little corner of the world, I issued an invitation from the front of our small church congregation. Knee-deep in the throes of full-time ministry, these were my people, and I wanted them to come, to break bread, to share life with me.

I chuckle now at my innocence. Although I shouldn't call it innocence because it didn't come from a heart of naiveté. What should I name it? Youthful devotion perhaps? Wholeheartedness? Either way, I'm envious of that young girl who gave spontaneously from a heart of pure, unadulterated joy without calculating a to-do list or timetable. My simple act of hospitality wasn't equated with any stress, hours of house cleaning, or budget-breaking buffets. I just wanted them to come. I wanted to gather people, and I didn't second-guess myself.

Oh, did I mention we lived in an eight-hundred-square-foot apartment? And that my pot of chili could only squeak out soup cups for fifteen? I wasn't ready for a crowd, but it didn't matter. They came anyhow, and seventy-five people spilled out of our little place onto the grass—spreading out on blankets, pulling lawn chairs up close, echoing with laughter.

Across the way was our widowed neighbor, whom I saw peeking through her window to check on the front-yard commotion. I waved her outside, "Join us! There's plenty." Something about that spontaneously simple invitation ministered to the heart of a woman who'd felt profound loss, and it served as a catalyst for a newfound friendship—not only that day but continuing forward over yard sale conversations and furniture restoration tips.

That day ignited my love of spontaneous hospitality. Yep, I'm a big fan of the last-minute invitation. I realize, if you're a planner, it might drive you a bit crazy, but think of the benefits: (a) it eliminates last-minute cancellations; (b) it cuts through all the back-and-forth attempts at coordinating calendars and busy schedules; and (c) it lowers expectations. No one envisions a big soiree. They're just anticipating a casual gathering of fun.

One of my favorite family traditions actually came about from a last-minute burst of spontaneity. I've always wanted to do a big Christmas party—it's such a festive time of year—but the busier we became as a family, we made an intentional decision to keep our December schedules slowed down. It was always hard to balance that with hosting a large Christmas gathering in the middle of it, plus I didn't want to set up expectations I couldn't fulfill.

But one year I got a wild idea. A few days before Christmas, I e-mailed invitations for an "after Christmas" open house. (I mentioned this concept briefly in a previous chapter.) Our home was still decorated for the holidays, right? No planning necessary there. People brought extra Christmas treats they didn't want in their house anymore, and I purchased all my paper products and party favors on December 26 when everything was marked down to half off. I enjoyed the big open house I'd always wanted without the pressure to perform. Spontaneity carried the day again.

Here are a few other spontaneous ideas we've implemented that I hope you'll try—*any* time of year.

- Invite your cul-de-sac to a root beer float party, or send a group text invitation for a "Popsicle and Pop-in" time or a snow day hot chocolate party.
- Host a spontaneous "Build Your Own _____ Bar" meal. Build your own ice cream bar, baked potato bar, burrito bar, pizza bar, or for a fancier occasion, try a bruschetta bar or mashed potato bar (served up in martini glasses for a dramatic flair). These work well for large groups, and everyone can bring a topping, which means minimal work for the host.
- Never underestimate the power of the grill. One of our most memorable nights came from an e-mail blast I sent out with twenty-four-hours' notice. I didn't think many would attend since it was July 3, but surprisingly many friends were available. We threw chicken and hot dogs on the grill, and everyone brought a side or dessert to share.
- Give an open invitation to a "Leftover Thanksgiving Meal on Black Friday." My friend shared this idea, which is especially great if you aren't able to gather with family for the weekend.
- "Come on Over for Some Nachos" party. Check my blog for my Dump and Run Taco Soup recipe. I always make extra to

freeze. Not only is it better the next day after the flavors meld, but the leftovers can be used as the main topping for your baked potato bar, as well as drizzled over tortilla chips for some gourmet nachos in minutes.

Here are two more from some (in)couraged readers:

Kerri—"We've started the tradition of 'Friday Night Pizza,' where we make dough from scratch (easy, frugal, and fun) and the invite is open-ended. We never know who will show up. They come at various times in the evening and often bring different gifts—soda, toppings, etc. But they know it's not required. After several months, they're almost trained to know they can drop in, but it's taken some real convincing. I still worry a teensy bit if the house is messy, but once we're talking and laughing, the clutter is forgotten."

Jamie—"Last week at the coffee shop, a college girl overheard me say where I attended high school decades ago. She turned to me and said, 'I went there, too.' She had moved to our town only five days earlier. Who doesn't need an invitation after five days? I asked if she'd like to come over for waffles and said I'd invite other college kids for her to meet. She came. We ate. She's a vegan. She still ate. And when she got ready to go, she asked, 'Do you do these waffle things a lot?' I told her no—but if she'd like to come, I'd do it again. And she said yes. She's due here this Saturday at 8:15. This time for blueberry-stuffed French toast. It's not the offering that matters. It's that you offer."

So there you have it. The sky is really the limit when your only goal is to gather people together, whether at home or away, whether summer or winter, whether ready or not. If you want to see God at work in creative ways, get creative with your spontaneous invitations. The workload is much easier, and the enjoyment can't be beat.

But let me tell you—planned, regular, thought-out, deliberate hospitality, offered up to God as a gift to Him and to others, is powerful enough to turn the whole trajectory of people's lives. Know how I know? Because of the people whose on-purpose hospitality has radically influenced me.

One of those people was Jan. (I mentioned her name to you along with several others in chapter 7, "The Power of One.") She modeled for me, along with some other young teenage girls, how to use food as a vehicle for hospitality. I was reminded of her impact on my life not long ago while sorting through some old dusty boxes. Stuck between jelly-stained pages of recipe cards and family cookbooks was a treasure trove I'd assumed was lost forever. I found all the recipes Jan had handwritten and mimeographed for us so we'd each have copies to take home. From enchiladas and Chinese chicken to basic brownies and chocolate cake, I can almost taste the meals we enjoyed together.

Oh, the memories that resurfaced as I pried those recipes loose from their confined corner. The carefree days of a sixteen-year-old catapulted back to the present. I distinctly remember the sense of feeling empowered when Jan—a fun, young mom—took four other high school girls and me under her wing. During a time in our lives when school, friends, boys, and parents triggered hours of emotional dumping, cloaked as discussion and dialogue, our weekly home gatherings served as a buoy keeping us afloat. A time when affirmation was currency and attention was the payment.

But then she decided to tweak our typical Bible study time by adding some cooking lessons. Throughout those summer months, she introduced us to new foods, new cooking techniques, and new kitchen tips. It definitely wasn't like your grandma's Bible study, although she took one of life's most simple pleasures from that bygone era—learning to cook from scratch—and intertwined it into foundational truths.

Every week she picked one meal for us to master—a main dish, side, and dessert. And as we chopped and mixed, folded and kneaded, not only did it awaken our creativity, but it allowed conversation to flow untethered by the constraints of a typical discipleship time.

As we chopped the veggies, she shared on the "dicey-ness" of marriage and the importance of putting time into making a marriage a true partnership. As we stirred, she shared wisdom on the swirling challenges of parenting. Then as the desserts baked, we gathered to talk about typical stresses we dealt with as senior-high students while she led us to Scriptures to help combat peer pressure.

I'll be honest, I don't remember anything too specifically from those discussions. I remember them making me feel more confident and encouraged. Or maybe the reason I don't remember is because I was always too excited to test out our culinary masterpieces on the special guests scheduled to arrive at any minute—the high school *guys'* small group who joined us as the meal finished. We'd pile our finished results on serving trays and then all enjoy eating them together. It doesn't get much better than that.

As weeks went by, we learned the art of appreciating simple ingredients—how they're useless by themselves, but when blended with other unimportant elements, a simple fare becomes a feast. We learned to slow down, to realize no matter how much we wanted to rush the process and race to the end, the joy was found in the journey. By embracing the process, even when it resulted in a few burned edges from mistakes made along the way, the end result was always worth the wait.

Those are the kinds of things Jan demonstrated to us, weaving discipleship and evangelism into the fabric of a unique experience. Those summer months together weren't about exchanging deep theological takeaways, but we all left with something even better: a safe place to learn and create, an open home where our hearts were heard, and a shared rite of passage—one generation equipping the next through tangible life skills that decades later now serve my own family well.

So as I pulled out this treasure of Jan's handwritten recipes, I was reminded that cooking and food aren't just about feeding stomachs. At their finest, they feed the soul. Food is about sharing life around a table—a table meant for food but also for so much more.

And I was reminded about the power of doing hospitality on purpose. Hospitality *with* a purpose.

My friend Debbie's annual Christmas Tea had a similar effect. A notable doctor's wife and businesswoman, she desired to steward her influence and used an afternoon of beauty and refreshment as the gateway to do so. The invitations acknowledged a festive time to gather, enjoy special music, and hear an inspirational message. As her neighbors, coworkers, female doctors, and the doctor's wives from her husband's practice gathered, she spoke life into their hearts acknowledging her story as one changed by His goodness. Evangelism served as the defined goal, but the creative and purposeful avenue used was an exquisite Christmas tea. As she elevated beauty in her home and pampered these women, all glory pointed to Him.

On purpose.

When our kids were little, I especially enjoyed evenings that held a *twofold* purpose for hospitality—fellowship alongside completing tasks. For years I hosted meal-making groups where we had a blast together but also left with eight meals finished and ready to cook. I started those evenings up again when our boys hit their teen years because dinnertime chaos kept winning, and I wanted to get back on my A-game. Why did I ever stop? The little bit of work up front is so worth having dinner ready for a few weeks. (Check out this idea and many other on-purpose hospitality options in this chapter's Elevate the Ordinary section.)

So I ask you again which is best:

A. Hospitality is best when it's spontaneous.

B. Hospitality is best when it's on purpose.

I think I can see you nodding your head. I can't wait to hear what ideas you come up with. Won't you let me know?

Dear Jen

I've heard you share about "Pigfest," and I've always wanted to attend. Can you share how this started? It fascinates me.

Curious

Dear Curious,

Yes, one of the finest examples of hospitality on purpose I've ever experienced is through an evening called "Pigfest," which my brother hosts. This evening, unlike any other, is for those ready to take hospitality and conversation to the next level. It involves learning to debate, to attack ideas without attacking a person, to humbly agree to disagree, and still part as friends.

For many of us, the art of listening, and then questioning, wasn't modeled for us, and therefore the masterpiece known as civil discourse has been lost. I would suggest the finest art of communication is in learning to listen with utmost humility, to attempt to really hear another's point of view, and then figuring out the questions to ask to draw out the thoughts of another. With my passion, empathy, and justice-oriented nature, I run the gamut of emotions at every Pigfest. But never do I leave without feeling stretched into a bigger, broader, stronger, humbler person, more convinced than ever that my faith in God is well placed. I've asked my brother to expand on it in the following Extra Helping.

Jen

Hosting Community Tables

When I was in high school, I rebelled against my parents and God. (Those two things usually go together.) It took someone inviting me to the table to get me reengaged in the light and life of faith.

The grey-haired host called it a "Pigfest." He pursued me, inviting me to come to a table prepared with love, piled high with food—including many great foods my mom wasn't serving! He explained the name of the event by saying the idea was to pig out on good food and good conversation.

I went for the food.

The gathering was an entirely new experience to me. People from seventeen to seventy "mealing" together, as they called it, talking about things that matter. The conversation was moderated by the host. The conversation was intentionally limited to five subjects: history, philosophy, politics and economy, culture, and theology.

Those attending could propose any question about something they believed to be important relating to one of those subjects. The host would facilitate conversation in fifteen-minute rounds, at the end of which an old-fashioned alarm bell would sound. The moderator would wrap up the exchange and then present the next question. And so on it went, throughout the meal, from appetizers until dessert (and often beyond).

I went to that first Pigfest for the food, but I went back again and again for the conversation. I realized few people set a gracious table where people from varied generations, with sometimes opposing ideologies, could gather and listen, learn and share. It lit the fire of learning in me again.

It also lit the fire of faith in me again. The Christian hospitality and the winsome hopefulness of the gospel as it brought light to every subject awakened me. I loved the Socratic approach (which, the host reminded us, did not belong to Socrates). Jesus, in fact, asked fifty-two questions in the book of Luke alone! He apparently thought highly of a pedagogy using thoughtful questions.

He liked to break bread at table too.

The host was full of life, sometimes pressing but always gracious. He worked hard to see that all present had a voice and that their voices were valued and considered. He connected things back to the gospel in ways that surprised and encouraged me. He never passed a basket for money. He never even asked me to bring a dish or a bag of chips.

He only asked me to pay it forward.

And that's what I've tried to do, by revisiting the impact the Pigfest had on my life and in the lives of others I came to know during that season. After spending some time at Oxford during business school, where time with tutors "at table" and meals with students "in hall" were required, I was left asking the question: Who's setting the tables in our culture?

In his farewell address, Ronald Reagan famously observed, "All great change in America begins at the kitchen table." Indeed, every culture needs to ask that question because whoever sets the tables has great influence in setting the course of our families and our futures. So I began to set the table and invite people to it, once a quarter, then once a month. I studied the formats of famous gatherings from the past like the Clapham Circles that William Wilberforce used in changing public opinion toward the British slave trade in the early 1800s. I borrowed principles like those employed by Ben Franklin in his weekly gatherings of The Junto Society.

One of the ideas borrowed was Franklin's Devil's Rule, which enabled anyone to assume a devil's advocate position at any time without announcing it. These and other guides helped us navigate away from ad hominem (against the person) arguments and evaluate ideas for truth's sake alone.

Our kids, like my wife and me, have learned a lot about hospitality, conversation, and culture-making through this journey. Together we've learned how to have thoughtful points of view, not just opinions. We've learned how to listen to (and love) people with whom we disagree. And we've learned how much we haven't figured out.

Pigfests have changed us. They've made us different people, and they've made us many unexpectedly lifelong friends. Maybe Pigfests—name them what you will—might change you and others too.

Elevate the Ordinary

❀ Stumped for ideas as to where to begin doing some hospitality on purpose? Sometimes you only need a few hints to get your creative juices flowing.

❀ *Meal-Making Groups.* Organize a few hours for a casserole exchange, a freezer cooking session, favorite cookbook recipes night, or "Mommas and Marinades."

❀ *Busy Bees' Night.* Guests bring anything they need to work on, such as addressing Christmas cards, organizing paperwork for taxes, finishing a scrapbook, writing a birthday letter to their kids, or even laundry to fold.

❀ *Makeup Tutorial Night.* Ask one friend who's fabulous at creating "smoky eyes" to teach your small group how to do it. Have everyone share favorite products and have fun playing with new techniques.

❀ *Spa Night.* Give one another manis and pedis.

❀ *Old-Fashioned Slumber Party.* For years, I kicked my family out and hosted a ladies' slumber party. While we splurged with a movie marathon, I remember one friend using our guest room and sleeping for ten hours straight. Must have been exactly what she needed, and I was glad to provide it for her.

❀ *Five Favorite Things Night.* Each guest brings five favorite things to share. It can be anything from beauty to household products, from kitchen hacks to an odd, unheard-of find.

❀ *Fun with Power Tools or Car Care Basics Class.* Enlist someone to share basic skills so you can discover your inner DIY or learn to add/change the oil.

❀ *Mother and Daughter Homemaking Skills.* Every month one mom offers to teach a skill she's mastered or perhaps find someone who can come in to teach a skill she may want to learn. We've had simple sewing, canning, homemade-bread baking, and a furniture painting class. Don't have a daughter? Perfect time to begin a mentoring relationship.

❀ *Craft Night.* Decorate Mason jars, do flower arranging, learn cake decorating, and more.

❀ *Exercise Together.* Invite friends to a "Fit and Fellowship" or "Stroll and Strollers" walking group in the park.

❀ *Bunco, Board Games, Cards*

❀ *Backyard Bible Club for Neighborhood Kids.* Moms *love* this because they get free childcare.

❀ *Neighborhood Yard Sale.* Get to know your street and declutter at the same time.

❀ *Christmas Cookie Exchange and Christmas Caroling.* Share music and plates of cookies.

❀ *Clothing and Accessory Swap.* Everyone brings something she doesn't wear anymore but is still cute and trendy.

❀ *Home Décor and Home Accessories Swap.* Can you tell I love to reuse and repurpose?

❀ *Movie Marathon.* Popcorn with the BBC version of *Pride and Prejudice*, anyone?

15

Hospitality Rooted in Adoption

'*ve never met her, yet her sacrifice of hospitality changed my life.
Seventeen—still a child herself. She must have been terrified. Not
to mention increasingly conflicted, the longer she shared a heartbeat
with the precious life being knit together in her womb. Yet on a blustery
Milwaukee March day, she made a choice.

A choice of sacrifice. A choice of redemption. A choice of hope.

Decades later, I sit at this computer pondering what that decision
means. It's not lost on me that I'm the recipient of one of the greatest
acts of hospitality one woman could do for another: the giving of life.
Her decision that day—both heroic and brave—has already affected
generations. Because of her hope for a better life for her daughter, God
has given me one of the greatest gifts I've ever received. I can't begin to
understand it. I don't know why I was chosen. Yet her decision to give
me over for adoption has changed my life.

Years later, when I became a mother myself, my heart ached for her. I
couldn't imagine—still can't—what it would be like never to know one's
firstborn. The idea of transferring that holy, sacred time to another is a
thought that breaks my heart in two. As she poured life from her womb,
she knew another mother's arms would soon be filled. As her heart shattered, mine formed. How can such an ironic dichotomy exist?

But not until our second son was born with a congenital disease
did my curiosity about her part in my story significantly grow. Until
then, I'd honestly never felt any real compulsion to search for my birth
mother. I'd never felt that empty, aching hole my university professor
warned about in psychology class. I remember feeling more frustration

than anything else as he covered the core issues that adopted children wrestle with, ranging from rejection and abandonment to loss of identity. None of those resonated with me. Even when dealing with my son's diagnosis, the "need to know" questions about my family medical history struck me initially on a logistical level, not an emotional one. Doctors were probing me with questions for which I didn't have the answers. I felt helpless and incomplete, only able to supply non-identifying, superficial information. Our son was sick, facing necessary surgery, and I didn't know my story.

This was the first time I truly started to wonder deeply about this woman who bore me years ago. I found myself thinking back to times in my childhood when young moms sometimes stayed in our home, asking me other questions I was equally unable to answer.

My parents' door was always open to people in need, including unmarried mothers seeking a place to live during their pregnancies. Thirty years ago, so much more than today, having a baby out of wedlock came with a shame-laced stigma. Girls needed a safe haven where they could escape when the doors of home and family were shut, and my parents graciously opened the door to a number of them. Knowing I was adopted, these girls often came to me for reassurances. I couldn't promise them anything, yet I heard the cry of each heart: "I hope I'm doing the right thing. Have you met your birth mom? Do you want to meet her? Please tell me this choice is best for my baby."

But in thinking through the unknowns about my own son's health and pondering again those agonizing questions from the soon-to-be mothers I'd met through the years, I began to formulate new questions of my own: *Could it be possible that the woman who gave me life has voiced these same thoughts? For decades? Does she wonder what's happened to her firstborn? Does she still hope she made the right decision?*

In some ways, these questions have never left me. Recently, I watched a movie where a birth mom was reunited with her daughter. In the gripping scene where they held each other for the first time, the mother sobbed, "I thought about you every single day." Surprisingly, yet almost reflexively, my heart grieved in a way I'd never experienced before. This gift that my own biological mother had given, which allowed me to grow up in a home wholly committed to knowing and following Jesus, is one I can never repay. For even as God "knit me together" inside her womb (Ps. 139:13), He saved the last stitching until six weeks after my birth, when the final bonding was done with my forever family. At just seventeen years old, one young woman's unselfish sacrifice opened the door so that I might know where my ultimate hope resides.

Through adoption, I received a new identity when my parents signed their name on the papers. That's a part of my own story that may or may not be part of yours. But more importantly, through the sacrifice of His Son on the cross, God adopted me into *His* forever family when I named Jesus as Lord and Savior. And every one of us can be on the receiving end of that story—the greatest adoption story ever told. As pastor and author John Piper is widely ascribed as saying, "The gospel is not a picture of adoption. Adoption is a picture of the gospel."

God set the example for what adoption should be—the welcoming of an outsider into the inner circle of a family. How can I not feel honored that I also get to live out a tangible representation of what's been infused on my heart since birth? My life is a result of the gift of hospitality, both physically and spiritually. A gift from the woman who birthed me but ultimately a gift from the Lord.

I pray, when thinking of her, "Precious Lord, does she who bore me know You? Does she have the same hope? I want her to know You, my Jesus—the Redeemer of our past mistakes and the hope for our future."

And so I "wait for the blessed hope, the appearing of the glory of our great God and Savior, Jesus Christ" (Titus 2:13), and I pray when that day comes, she will be there—the woman who gave me life. I will introduce her to my devoted parents, and together our chorus will simply echo, "Thank you."

For a choice of sacrifice. A choice of redemption. A choice of hope.

My heart overflows with gratitude for this woman's choice. I can't imagine my life if it were any different. As I mentioned, the practice of opening the door to other women who were facing a similar choice was something modeled to me by my parents early in my life.

So I'd like to share with you my friend's viewpoint as one of the young girls who was welcomed into our home and family at a critical point in her life. I've added a few comments, which you'll see, but listen for how my mom and dad's Christlike hospitality took this woman from heartache to hopefulness and healing.

Roughly thirty years ago I made a life-changing decision and found myself unmarried, pregnant, and thousands of miles away from home. The father didn't want our child and was pushing me to abort her. Eventually I decided to make choices that prioritized the needs of my child and me, and that meant I needed to get away from him.

My mom and sister picked me up from the airport, but it quickly became apparent that I would not be able to stay at my parents' house during my pregnancy. Their shame and fear of being judged for having a pregnant, unmarried daughter were overwhelming for all of us. I had no support system and was unsure what to do next.

At church the next Sunday, a representative of a Christian adoption agency spoke. After the service I talked with him about my decision to carry my baby to term, wanting to see her placed with another family. He said the agency was willing to help me in any way they could, including helping me find an apartment. But he also mentioned the name of a family who supported the agency. They had an adopted daughter, he said, and he felt sure they would welcome me into their home if I felt comfortable with that arrangement.

I decided to meet this family and move forward, given the strain my pregnancy was having on my family, especially my mom. Plus I was lonely, and I wanted to be with a family. "God," I prayed with great hope and anticipation, "is this what You have for me?"

When I met them, we sat together and talked as they expressed their gratitude for their adopted daughter. They continued to tell me that opening their home and their lives to me would be an honor, a way for them to give back after they'd been blessed through their own experience with adoption. I felt loved and welcomed immediately and accepted their invitation, a gift of moving into their home and into their hearts . . . into their family. As I experienced God's love and kindness through them, I settled in. I was in a caring place, thriving emotionally and physically.

We marveled at how well God worked out all the details. I settled into a job, we laughed together, we talked, we ate meals together, and I became part of their family by doing normal family activities. I felt more like a sister than an outsider. Vandy and I were inseparable. *(Vandy is my mother's nickname.)* We mutually adored one another.

Their daughter Jenny *(that's me)* was only fifteen at the time. She was unhindered and so comfortable with herself. She would plop down at the piano to play and sing out loud whether anyone was listening or not. She looked so much like her mom and brothers that it was hard to believe she was adopted. Watching her live her life showed me that adopted children are loved and can do well in their adopted homes. Jenny flourished with the loving guidance of her parents.

Still, it was a difficult and trying time for me. Outwardly, I appeared to be thriving. Inwardly, however, I felt such great pain. At night I would talk to my baby girl, imagine holding her, and tell her how much I loved her. Knowing the day was coming soon that I would give birth to this precious baby growing inside of me made it worse. How could I give her to an unknown couple? I clung to the hope God was giving me that my baby would fit in with her adopted parents, just as Jenny did.

And He truly saw me through. Even now it's sometimes difficult to look back, but I feel as if I did the right thing.

I don't know if I could have done it, though, if not for the family who selflessly gave me house and home, treating me like I belonged in their family. I became the recipient of the most extreme acts of hospitality. My life was forever changed during this time. I saw a husband who loved and honored his wife, a true team, praying together and creating an atmosphere of unity, peace, and love, which demonstrated healthy boundaries for their children.

We've stayed in touch all these decades, and I've seen how this life of hospitality has been passed down through the generations to their children's families and their children's children.

Isn't this what God does for us? He invites us in and loves us first.

The gift of adoption continued in our family when I met Edison eight years ago. It was love at first sight. What a life-changing gift I was granted when my sister-in-law asked me to accompany her to Ecuador to bring him home from the orphanage to be with his forever family. As his adopted aunt, I found it not only one of my greatest privileges but divine providence to bring this generational marker of adoption full circle.

Since we live next door to each other, I've had a front-row seat to their adoption journey, one that began with a four-year battle. A fight not just against political red tape and legislation but a spiritual battle against the powers of good and evil. Many times we didn't think he'd join our family.

People label Eddie as special needs, but the truth is that he is a special blessing to everyone in need that he meets. Almost daily, this miracle comes traipsing through our woods to see us. He loves big. He eats big. But most importantly he loves with honesty, purity of heart, and a passion he pours into every person he greets. *Whether they want it or not.* He is so full of love to share.

When people found out that my brother and sister-in-law were pursuing adoption, many voiced the opinion that they were crazy to adopt another child into an already large family. "You have your hands full enough already. Why would you do this?"

Leave it to my brother Jim to have the perfect answer:

According to the police report, which I carry daily, Edison was discovered by a "carpenter" who heard the sound of a baby crying from inside a trash bag, left to die on the outskirts of the city dump.

Left to die—found by a carpenter.

That's my story; that's our story.

In a spiritual sense I'm the kid in the trash bag on the outskirts of the dump, discovered by the Carpenter. That Carpenter pursued me and made me worthy to be His son through His great sacrifice on my behalf.

So how could I do any less for another orphan, like me?

This little boy with Down syndrome is a critical, strategic part of our estate plan. In this fight for the culture of life, he is a special emblem of all that is good and precious and now is right in the middle of our family—a remarkably special person who speaks into the lives of our children and others we meet and ultimately points us to Christ.

What a stunning journey—meandering through the years. Rachel has said this was her hardest delivery yet (the others are natural born). But as we see Edison light up so many homes and dole out thousands of hugs and kisses as if he were our designated ambassador of love, we are deeply grateful—grateful to God for this boy's preciousness, grateful to the orphanage for their loving care, grateful to our family and friends who prayed him home and helped in so many other ways, and grateful for our new life together!

As I think back on Eddie's life-giving impact, every turned page whispers God's grace in miraculous ways.

As I think back on my own story, I see God's unrelenting grace transforming sin and shame into an absolute miracle, a life destined to bring Him glory.

As I think back on my birth mother's devoted, full-term, sacrificial bravery, I'm humbled and grateful for what one person can truly do for another.

As I think back on my mom's compassion for the hurting young girls who've found refuge in my parents' home, I'm inspired to take my place in this legacy of caring.

And as I think backward and forward on my life with Christ and my adoption so undeserved by the Father, I'm amazed all over again at what the gospel means, what the gospel does, and what the gospel enables broken, needy people to receive. And to give.

Dear Jen

I know how important adoption is, and Scripture tells us to take care of the orphans. We aren't planning on adoption, but how can I encourage those who are in the process?

How Do I Help?

Dear How Do I Help,

Your heart for encouragement is wonderful. Many people read James 1:27 and don't engage with its importance because they aren't planning to adopt, yet we have the opportunity to partner with these families in a significant way to help care for orphans. The adoption process is extensive, in terms of both time and financial resources. Opportunities abound for helping adoptive families with miscellaneous expenses or by offering child care while they work on their home study or during their travels, if adopting internationally.

I've asked my dear friend Vanessa Hunt, author of *Life in Season,* to share some ideas. After struggling with infertility, she and her husband felt led to adopt their two children. Here's the kind of help she found most effective as people came alongside them throughout the adoption process.

Vanessa writes:

- Offer to host a shower so they have all the same things parents would receive if they had a biological child.
- Start a meal train so the family can have time to bond together without having to worry about cooking.
- Find an adoption-specific baby book or memory book (so many of these are available now!) to give the family. They will love

getting to fill in the details of their special journey to share with their child someday.

- Remember that you don't have the right to know all of the details of the adoption, since some may be confidential. Refrain from asking prying questions. Instead, ask how you can pray for them.

- I might not have grown my children in my belly, but I grew them in my heart, and once we adopted them, we joined the ranks of new parents. Make sure you include adoptive families in playdates, moms' groups, and other activities.

- Be understanding and respectful of the time it often takes for adoptive families to bond, especially when older children are adopted. They may need to drop out of sight for a while, and that's okay!

Jen

Elevate the Ordinary

❀ Create your own family mission statement or family logo. Refer to its significance often. We took the first initial of our five children to make "T.E.A.M. D." Our family is a team, and win or lose, we persevere and work together.

❀ On Mother's Day, send a message or send something special to a friend dealing with infertility, miscarriage, or loss of a child. Take a second now to add her name to your calendar and set it to remind you. These women grieve silently, and these mile-marker days are difficult.

16

The Uncomfortable Yes

"Jen, it's about Johnny. He has a brain tumor. They think it's malignant. They're doing surgery shortly."

You've gotten that call, I'm sure—if not that one, a similar one that's equally urgent and upsetting. By virtue of being in relationship with another person, whether through family or church or a connection of shared acquaintance, you've entered immediately into someone else's season of grief, trial, and suffering. Few people are ever ready for it when it happens to them.

But neither are those—like you, like me—who wish to walk alongside them through it, as we did for my brother who was dealing with this disturbing news about his son. When life is hard, what should you say? What should you do? How do you serve them in a way that's enough but not too much? Helpful but not intrusive? How do you meet a real need without unintentionally creating a burden? How do you most effectively take worries off their mind so they can concentrate unhindered on what's most important?

I watched people minister to my brother's family in profound ways over the next few months, following this shocking, devastating interruption to their lives. Many compassionate friends and even strangers stepped into an uncomfortable situation and said yes to being the hands and feet of Jesus.

And over a lifetime of both observing and receiving this kind of life-giving service in a variety of challenging circumstances, as well as attempting to provide it myself, I've learned some critical and practical lessons. My hope is that the suggestions in this brief chapter will change the way you do life for others in crisis, just as they've changed us. I pray they'll help you see that a heart of hospitality means showing up for the most difficult times, willing and available.

Ideas for Helping Others in Crisis

Anticipate Needs and Be Specific

If I've learned one thing in light of anticipating needs, it's to *act now*. Do not wait. Do not offer. Just do it! In the past, even though my heart ached to help, I'd fall back on the familiar words, "Please let me know if you need anything." Now I realize this sentiment must turn into action.

A person in crisis is in survival mode. Don't place them in the difficult position of having to filter through and access what they need, followed by reaching out to you and asking. When life is swirling and they're just struggling to maintain, thinking through a list of past offers is nearly impossible. Analysis paralysis sets in, and most people will never ask for help.

Give Spiritual Encouragement

"I'm praying for you" is a fine thing to say, but it's a phrase that often gets lost. I don't want to be one of those who just shares it while passing in the aisle at church. I want to follow through when it really matters.

Instead of mentioning, "I'm praying for you," take it a step further and write out a specific prayer or Scripture that the Lord brought to you and give it to your friend, either in person or by text or e-mail.

In moments of crisis, God hears our groaning, but our weary minds may not be able to bring Scripture to the forefront. Being able to meditate on God's truth written on good old-fashioned note cards is a lifeline. Rereading Scriptures and personal prayers is something pretty special. It tells them a band of prayer warriors is truly standing in the gap and interceding on their behalf.

Another source of God's truth that helps ward off doubt is praise and worship music. Consider creating a topical playlist specific to their needs. Everyone can be encouraged and uplifted while worship plays in the background of their hospital room.

Give Physical Nourishment

When moments of crisis hit, the first thing people think of is providing meals. Identifying a family's need in that area is critical, but often it takes a few days to set up a meal train.

For my brother's family, a tangible blessing came instantaneously when their pastor's wife filled their fridge with all the necessities. She didn't ask. She just did it. A stocked fridge spoke to their love language, and having a few freezer meals set aside specifically for those in need is a goal of mine. Some of our easy favorites are taco casserole, easy baked ziti, and slow cooker buffalo chicken.[15]

My dear friend Tammy, whom we hadn't seen for months, brought Chick-fil-A to the hospital waiting room for our entire extended family. She anticipated this need, and even after I repeatedly told her no, she showed up anyhow. We didn't anticipate how much we'd need something other than cafeteria food during surgery time, but *she* did. If she had called and asked, "What can I do for you?" I would have assured her we were just fine because I thought we were.

Create Hospital Survival Kits

My sweet friend Siobhan put together "emergency bags" for the whole family. I now call them Hospital Survival Kits because she thought of everything we needed to survive for a weeklong hospital stay. Blankets (and a prayer shawl), slippers, lip balm and lotion, quarters for the vending machines, toothbrushes, toothpaste, floss, wipes, deodorant, healthy snacks, protein bars, meals to heat up in the microwave, drinks, and water are some of the things those blessing bags contained. Such a practical idea that anyone can do, but often we don't. I want to be that proactive person.

While each of these situations is different, there is never a bad time to show acts of service. Clean a bathroom, drop off paper products at the house (toilet paper, paper towels, napkins), do a load of laundry, get the oil changed in their car. Whispering a word of encouragement ministers to a weary heart above and beyond the appreciation expressed. Be available. Share your presence, if even for a few minutes, while always being sensitive to the situation, knowing at times the family will need to regroup and be left alone.

Every day the Lord opens the door for us to step through it and offer up our uncomfortable yes to Him. What will yours be today?

Dear Jen

A friend of mine recently lost her baby at eighteen months. I never know what to say or do after a death. It's different from a hospital stay. Do you have suggestions?

Grieving

Dear Grieving,

I've asked my precious friend Tammy to weigh in with a few suggestions that help us step forward in our discomfort. While my nephew Johnny miraculously recovered, Tammy knows how it feels when things end differently. She lost her son Riley and still walks this road of grieving eight hundred days later. Yes, they count the days; it's part of the process. She ministers to me on a regular basis with her vulnerability and truth. She's the friend who points me to see life in a new way, and she's also the one who met us in our own hospital waiting room with Chick-fil-A sandwiches.

Remember: I don't *have* to; I *get* to.

Since she lives with grief every day, her first-person perspective gives us a glimpse of its importance. Tammy writes:

• *Pray.* Storm the gates of heaven for the soul of your friend. Implore Jesus to help her so she will not fall away from the faith. The enemy will be on the prowl when she is at her lowest, and she will need prayer partners waging war for her.

• *Bring food.* She will need sustenance for herself and her family (sometimes months later). Simple, comfort food is best. And cookies.

• *Share photos and memories of her loved one.* She wants to hear all the good things you can say about the person she's lost. One of the best cards I received when my son died was from a mom of three boys. She listed her sons' favorite memories of my son—times when he'd been kind to them or made them feel included. It was precious.

• *Give her meaningful jewelry.* It was vital for me to wear things that connected me to my son who'd died. The first few days after he passed, I had to wear his clothes and his bracelet and sleep with his pillow. It was a means of survival, of going on without him, that I cannot fully explain. On the day of his burial, my beautiful friend gave me a necklace with photos of him with our family and me. I knew she had put thought, time, emotion, and love into designing and buying that necklace. It expressed everything a grieving mother needed without saying a word. It was perfect.

• *Do their chores without asking, especially yard work.* Grief is mentally and physically exhausting. Cutting someone's grass or raking their leaves is unobtrusive and will express your love in a tangible way.

• *Be creative.* I lost my son, but I still had to be a mother to his surviving siblings. My good friend was so clever to pack a bag of premade lunches for my daughter for school. She knew her well enough to know she loves strawberries and pretzels. I can still remember looking down in that bag and being so thankful that lunches were done for the week.

• *Plant flowers or trees in memory of the loved one.* We were allowed to plant a dogwood near my son's headstone, and it's been a tremendous blessing to watch it grow and change with the seasons. We tend to it regularly and decorate it for holidays. Friends and family have placed objects of love and remembrance on or around it. We also have trees and shrubs planted at our house in his memory. Nineteen beautiful rose bushes for nineteen beautiful years.

• *Be gentle with your words.* Don't tell her things like, "God knows best." This might be good theology, but she doesn't need theology when her heart is splayed open.

• *Keep texting words of encouragement.* Continue praying for her and for her wounded family. She needs her sisters and brothers in Christ to love her through the initial shock, the hard weeks that follow, the excruciating first holidays and birthdays, and all the sad days in between without her child here on this earth.

• *Perhaps most importantly, weep with her.* Check your dignity and well-applied mascara at the door and be ready to fully invest in her grief. This is not for the faint of heart. If you are afraid of embarrassing yourself, then just drop off the food and scurry out. One of the purest forms of compassion is found in hurting when someone else hurts. She will not be put off by your tears. I remember an older gentleman stopping by my house on a Sunday afternoon to offer his condolences. He held my hand with tears streaming down his face, telling me of the times he almost died as a young man. By the grace of God, he had dodged the effects of fast cars and careless behavior. He was almost apologetic that he had lived so long when my son did not. It was brave of him to be so vulnerable with me. Be willing to venture down into the valley of death's shadows, down in the trenches. Be willing to weep.

• *And also, don't expect your old friend.* She died with her child. A grieving mother will never be the same person again. Give her a long, long time before you try to engage in small talk. Everyday, ordinary problems do not register with her anymore. It will be hard for her to focus, and she might forget everything you just said. And if she keeps canceling your lunch plans, forgive her.

Jen

17

Hospitality as Worship: The Ministry of Presence

She clutched the coffee cup, fingers intertwined, tears streaming down her face. The air sat heavy around us, a silent vapor settling deep. Inside of an hour, our relationship had quickly moved from "Hi, how are you?" acquaintance status to sisters, with hearts woven into a kinship known only through a shared story of struggle.

"I know this is going to sound ridiculous," she said, "and I don't mean for it to sound weird, but I've wanted to be friends with you for years."

With me? Based on her runway model good looks, her successful job, and her winsome personality, I figured she had her pick of friends. And I didn't picture myself as having whatever would put me high on that list.

She must have seen the "Really?" written on my face. "When you mentioned getting coffee, I thought it was a passing gesture. Then you e-mailed me your phone number and told me to text or call you anytime. I couldn't believe you followed through."

"Well, I'm so glad you could come."

"Actually, Jen, when you invited me over and set the date, . . . I started crying," she said, words that brought tears to her eyes even as she spoke them. Stumped, I couldn't fathom where this conversation was heading. This gorgeous woman in front of me appeared to have the ideal life, not one that would lend itself to getting emotional at being with me in such a simple, ordinary setting. I refilled her coffee while she found her voice again.

"No one knows all that's happening with me," she said, as tears continued falling freely. "I haven't left my house in weeks. I took a leave of absence from work and have been having these severe panic attacks. Even when I woke up this morning, my heart felt like it was caving in at the thought of coming to your house. I'm embarrassed to admit it, but that's just how it's been with me lately. The internal back-and-forth battle of knowing I needed (and wanted) to come was paralyzing. My mind kept telling me not to go.

"But it's the first time I've felt a sense of joy and anticipation in a long time," she went on. "I need community and I want friends. It's just been so hard. I've been so afraid to put myself out there. Sometimes the rejection isn't worth it."

I sat stunned. How had I so misjudged her? Mentally, the problem fixer in me started making a list of WWJD responses. What Bible verse could I share? How could I comfort her when this was so outside my realm, and when—again, honestly, *Why me?* Why had she entrusted her heart with me? And how could I begin to steward her trust in a way that honored the Lord and honored my new friend? I was at a loss.

But here's why I've chosen to let you in on this moment: I knew the best I had to offer her was simply to be *present*. Sometimes that's enough. In fact, sometimes it's the perfect response, the best of all options. Sometimes the people before us just need us to be silent. And honestly, I struggle with silence. But her deep ache couldn't be fixed through my words. What she felt could only be fully remedied by the master Healer.

So I sat. I listened. I grabbed her hand and looked her in the eyes. I slid over the Kleenex box. I refilled her coffee mug and listened some more. Every once in a while, she'd ask for my words, but I kept them few. All she really needed was the ministry of my presence. She needed listening ears, a heart tender to receive her, and the knowledge that in these moments nothing was more important to me than being fully engaged in our time together.

When it did come my time to talk, I could only say, "I don't know where to start because I feel any of my words will sound trite." So I chose them carefully. "One thing I know to be true is that you are loved, and no one understands your grief, your panic, or your suffering more than Jesus. I can tell you, too, that I am here for you. And with you. And for as long as you'd like to stay, you are welcome. We have all afternoon."

Before long, we moved to the kitchen. She hadn't planned on staying for lunch, but it was a natural extension of our time together. Excusing myself for a second, before rummaging around in the fridge for some lettuce to wash and a few eggs to boil, I shot a quick text to cancel an afternoon appointment. Then I switched my phone off and returned. Soon the tears dried and laughter began.

She diced the carrots. I chopped the broccoli. She shared a bit more about her family while I wondered aloud how our paths had never crossed before. I cut the eggs, sprinkled them on the salad, and started mixing the dressing.

Then somewhere between all the chopping, dicing, and mixing, my bone-weary journey joined hers. As she struggled to put voice to her wounds, it unearthed my own. "I can't begin to understand everything you're going through," I'd already told her, "but I do understand how a deep sense of loneliness feels." There in each other's presence, as I sought to minister to *her*, the Lord used the vulnerability we'd created as a way of ministering to *me*.

I still don't know how it happened—how a simple coffee invitation between two relative strangers opened the door to this authentic mingling of spirits: a sacred space created where boundaries were destroyed and defenses diffused. I only know, through the ministry of presence, the Holy Spirit swept in, opened our hearts, took hold of any preconceived agenda, and gave us a glimpse into how the early church practiced hospitality. I understood it even more intimately now, why it was so central to the biblical narrative. I sensed God's presence in the practice of it, where both host and guest received blessings of abundance.

Here we were, the two of us doing church curled up on my sofa sipping coffee. One of the root words of *hospitable* stems from the Latin's *hospitalia*. Or hospital. How appropriate. We had moved our prayer time to my kitchen, worshipped over a cutting board, then culminated with study at the table. And experienced healing.

As we hugged good-bye, and as I watched her drive away, exhaustion settled through my bones. Emotionally and physically emptied, I had poured out all that was available. I'd offered up what little I had to give, seeking to model our Savior, who chose in His infinite grace and mercy to pour out all He had for us. What I didn't expect was that as I emptied myself, He would refill.

It was the purest form of hospitality I'd experienced: an act of worship.

The ministry of *our* presence, inviting the ministry of *His*.

That afternoon marked another significant perspective shift in how I viewed hospitality. And as I close this book where we've journeyed from tornado parties, to last-minute invites, to pound cake recipes, to openhearted tales of home, friends, and fellowship, as well as the wealth of biblical frameworks that make hospitality both obedient and beautiful—or as I like to say, truly generation changing—I want to land here.

On worship.

That day wasn't a Hallmark moment defined by friends eating yummy treats, swapping recipes and home décor tips (although we slid a few of those in by the end). It was primarily marked by a holy time of worship. Our time together was aimed at the glory of God: to know Him and make Him known. It's where I began to see my offering of hospitality as a sacrificial act of worship.

As I dove later into some Scriptures on the topic, my heart recalibrated how I approached this gift of welcome we've all been given. To radically offer up our lives as a willing sacrifice, "holy and pleasing to God," is our "true and proper worship" (Rom. 12:1 NIV). To love others in such a tangible way in response to God's command—it's *worship*. Doesn't mean there's not a cost to be counted. And, yes, sacrifice is definitely involved. But the leading motivation, the driving force, is a desire to worship God through giving ourselves. And the joy that comes from this obedience to Him makes it well worth it.

It's always worth it!

Oh, sister, does this idea of "hospitality as worship" shift your view on welcoming others the way it did mine? It's shattered my image of needing perfect lives and perfect spaces. When I witnessed how a cup of coffee offered to a distant acquaintance could overflow into worship and healing, I realized biblical hospitality is much more than our latest dinner party. It's not always cozy, tame, and comfortable. I guess I'd describe it as broken people breaking bread with other broken people, laying it down at a table laden with grace. A redemption table reflecting God's glory. That's how I felt that day. Unsettled. Disrupted. Jesus did it in the best way possible. He disrupted my complacency and rerouted my dependency. He showed me again that to avoid the risk is to avoid the reward.

Do you remember my heart for this book? I started with an invitation to reshape how you view hospitality. I wanted to throw out the perfect hostess expectations and replace them with something that brings kingdom relevance to our hearts and homes. Honestly, I don't know if we'll ever truly understand hospitality as an act of worship until we open the door when we are completely empty, unequipped, and convinced we have nothing to offer. By making space to dig deep into both the joy and sorrow of others, we give ourselves margin to experience the most important things. Opening the door when we aren't ready defines hospitality in the deepest sense of the word. It's the exact place He wants us, and He guarantees He'll walk right to the door with us.

So how do we find the courage to step into the risk in order to experience the reward? We bring to the table our pride, we bring to the table our need for control, we bring to the table our trust issues, and we bring to the table our desired dependence on Him.

When we choose to bring our whole self fully poured out at the table, we bring our surrender and sacrifice to His altar. Once we've laid it all down, He picks it up, shifts it, and refines it. And when He hands it back, those blessings, the joy of open-door living—they're all worship.

Hospitality as worship.

All for You, Lord.

Notes

1. Martha Stewart, *Entertaining* (New York: Clarkson N. Potter, 1998).

2. "Our Favorite: Dump & Run Taco Soup," Balancing Beauty & Bedlam, accessed November 18, 2017, http://beautyandbedlam.com/easy -family-recipe-taco-soup.

3. C. S. Lewis, *Mere Christianity* (New York: Macmillan, Touchstone edition, 1996).

4. *Come and see* (John 1:39). *Follow Me* (Matt. 4:19). *Come and eat* (Luke 17:7). *Walk with Me* (John 8:12). *Sit with Me* (Mark 14:32). *Rest* (Matt. 11:28). *Drink* (John 7:37).

5. Oswald Chambers, *My Utmost for His Highest* (Grand Rapids, MI: Discovery House, 2017).

6. "A Third of Americans Have Never Met Their Neighbors," Science of Us, accessed November 18, 2017, http://nymag.com/scienceofus/2015/08 /third-of-americans-dont-know-their-neighbors.html.

7. Jay Pathak and Dave Runyon, *The Art of Neighboring* (Grand Rapids, MI: Baker, 2012), 36.

8. Leonard Sweet, *From Tablet to Table* (Colorado Springs: NavPress, 2015).

9. "Eating Alone: The Food Marketer's Hidden Opportunity," Hartman Group, accessed November 19, 2017, http://www.hartman-group.com /hartbeat/446/eating-alone-the-food-marketer-s-hidden-opportunity.

10. Robert Karris, *Eating Your Way through Luke's Gospel* (Collegeville, MN: Liturgical Press, 2006).

11. Jean Leclerc, quoted in Sweet, *From Tablet to Table*.

12. Tim Chester, *A Meal with Jesus* (Wheaton, IL: Crossway, 2011).

13. Ibid.

14. Check out my blog at www.beautyandbedlam.com, which highlights family traditions and ideas for every month of the year.

15. Recipes found at www.beautyandbedlam.com.

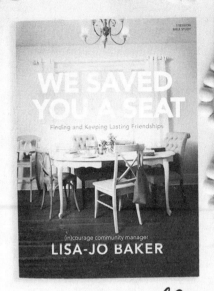

Jen Schmidt

For the last decade, Jen Schmidt has been encouraging, challenging, and cheering on women to embrace both the beauty and bedlam of their everyday lives on her popular lifestyle blog, *Balancing Beauty and Bedlam.*

With a variety of topics from easy dinner ideas and personal finance to leaving a legacy, Jen equips others to live life to its fullest, reminding them it's the little things that really are the big things in life.

A popular speaker, worship leader and founder/host of the annual Becoming Conference, Jen shares with humor and authenticity as she invites others to join her on this bumpy, beautiful life journey.

She lives in North Carolina with her husband, five children, a few too many animals and an available sofa for anyone who needs it.

Instagram:
Jenschmidt_beautyandbedlam

Facebook:
www.facebook.com/beautyandbedlam

Twitter:
@beautyandbedlam

For free resources, speaking inquiries and ideas for all things *heart* and *home:*

beautyandbedlam.com

(in)courage

FIND YOURSELF AMONG FRIENDS

To say *we love community* might be an understatement.

At (in)courage, our hearts beat for strong, healthy, God-honoring friendship.

Nothing brings us more joy than watching like-hearted women *connect.*

Connecting with others lightens the load and adds space for more laughter — and healing — because we know

we aren't alone.

Join us at **www.incourage.me** and connect with us on social media!

@incourage

A Study of Biblical Hospitality

Just Open
the Door

BIBLE STUDY

(in)courage author
JEN SCHMIDT

DAY TWO

See! I stand at the door and knock. If anyone hears my voice and opens the door, I will come in to him and eat with him, and he with me.

REVELATION 3:20

When we brainstormed the title for this book, I'll admit that this verse initially didn't cross my mind. Perhaps your first assumption gravitated to literal doors, because when you read the words "hospitality" and "door" on the same book cover, what else would you think?

Any entertaining expert would encourage us to put our best feet forward to make a good first impression, and that begins with our door, the gateway to our home.

Clear the clutter from the front porch. *Check.*

Hang a beautiful wreath. *Check.*

Arrange the entryway so it's warm and inviting. *Check.*

As we read yesterday about the orderly account of creation, we know God is in the smallest of details and created beauty for us to enjoy, but His primary focus has always been on the condition of our hearts.

> Humans do not see what the LORD sees, for humans see what is visible, but the LORD sees the heart.
> **1 SAMUEL 16:7b**

As I became more intimately acquainted with the Bible verses surrounding the heart of hospitality, I expanded my thought process to include "door" as a metaphor.

"Just Open the Door" doesn't always mean our personal home. If we're going to understand the full heart of the gospel, we must begin by asking the Lord to open the door of our hearts and soften it to reveal the needs around us. He wants to do this for us. He's opened my eyes in new ways. He's perked my ears to conversations that I typically stroll by, and He's revealing powerful stories simply because I'm slowing down enough to open the door wherever I am.

He's reminded me that every encounter matters to Him, no matter how small it might appear. And let me tell you, when I pray and plead that He'll soften my heart to reveal needs, He does it all right … every single time. It's up to me how I'll act on them.

So when we landed on this title, I sensed Him reminding me of its primary importance through Revelation 3:20. *Jen, this is what it's all about. If they'd just open the door to Me, they'll experience joy and fullness of life that they never knew existed.* In a surprising role reversal, God who began as the host, now awaits the most important invitation of all.

Can a simple invitation really change lives? Oh yes! We open the doors of our homes so we can point others to Him. We open the doors of our hearts and invite Him to be Lord of our lives. Continuously, we see that modeled in Scripture.

Beginning in the Old Testament, God tells His people to welcome and love the stranger. Within the context of that ancient culture, He instructed them to give of their time, energy, and whatever meager possessions were on hand, demonstrating hospitality to traveling strangers by feeding and housing them after an exhausting journey.

	Who offered hospitality? To whom?	What did they do for their guest?
Genesis 18:1-8		
Genesis 24:31		
Leviticus 23:22		
2 Samuel 17:27-29		
1 Kings 17:10-15		

What theme are you sensing?

How can we practically apply these verses to our lives today?

Did you know that the necessity of hospitality was actually part of their Mosaic Law? Yes, it was the law! Yikes! When I look at how our generation has become increasingly more individualistic and isolated creatures of comfort, I've asked myself how much trouble would I have been in back then?

It was not only the host's expectation to house, offer food, wash their feet, and keep guests from harm, it was an obligation. And these acts were always reciprocal in nature. Considered a breach of honor if either the host or the guest refused, strangers were welcomed as guests and might leave as friends. Communities lived interconnected, and their safety and survival depended on the kindness of strangers.

Hospitality in the ancient world focused on the stranger in need. The plight of aliens was desperate. They lacked membership in the community, be it tribe, city-state, or nation. As an alienated person, the traveler often needed immediate food and lodging. Widows, orphans, the poor, or sojourners from other lands lacked the familial or community status that provided a landed inheritance, the means to make a living, and protection. In the ancient world, the practice of hospitality meant graciously receiving an alienated person into one's land, home, or community and providing directly for that person's needs.

The kindness of strangers — it can be a lifeline when we most need it, can't it? One that doesn't need to be reserved for our Old Testament history class or the local nightly news.

> **Can you think back on a time when you've been the stranger, the new girl at work or home, or the uninvited guest who waited on the fringes for a word of welcome? Tell about that experience. Has it impacted how you reach out to others?**

Mine was very unconventional, but never have I needed a lifeline so desperately than when I was a college student traveling by myself through Europe. On my way to Bible school with my travel plans derailed, I stood alone in a London train station, wondering where I could lay my head for the next two evenings. Pulling out my list of approved youth hostels, I balanced the dial-up phone (yes, it was a few years ago), my coin purse (back when we needed to insert them every few minutes), and all the adventurous spirit I could muster. Always one to see the glass half full, I made my first call. No answer. *No problem. Lots more options await.* On to the second call. Sorry, no room. *No worries, there are six more to go.*

Painstakingly, I made my way down the list, but call by call ended with no availability. Ten o'clock at night, jet lagged, travel weary, and a stranger in a foreign land, I flipped to the last listed number, as my prior "conquer the world" nerves began crumbling.

An older woman answered. I requested a space, any space, and when she replied that they too were full, I did what any self-respecting girl might do. I begged. I pleaded. I told her I didn't care if I slept on the floor, but I was alone, I had no idea where I was, and I didn't have a place to stay.

"Please, can you help me?"

Friend, it was complete and utter desperation.

"We are completely full," the owner replied, "but I guess if you don't mind sharing a bed with Mary, she would be OK with it."

Share a bed with Mary? I didn't know Mary, but I felt an immediate kinship with her, because I'm fairly certain that when Jesus' mother's only choice was to sleep near the animals, she wasn't about to complain.

"Yes, thank you. Thank you," I replied as a strong sense of peace washed over me. Decades later as I recall that story, those emotions still rush to the forefront of my memory and I'm there in that phone booth once again.

Hailing the nearest taxi, I headed to the given address. As I was greeted by the very proper British proprietor, I lunged into her arms to show my appreciation — so American of me — and my next act still has me chuckling when I think back on this time. I climbed into bed with a complete stranger, better yet, a sleeping stranger. Now granted, sweet, elderly Mary was a retired missionary, and completely safe, or so I'm told, but yes, not only was I welcomed by a stranger, but I slept beside one too.

Recounting this story now, it sounds absolutely crazy. But I think it lines up perfectly with God's plan for offering hospitality to those strangers in need, and I guarantee, I was in need.

All these years later, I can't picture the face of the woman who showed me such kindness, but her extended gift of an invitation became a lifeline when I needed it most. It felt radical to this overwhelmed traveler who desperately yearned for someone to offer grace and extend a simple welcome.

Have you had a similar experience of welcome? Tell about how you were made to feel at home.

This experience marked me in such a profound way that my heart for the stranger, the lonely girl, the one waiting on the outskirts to be invited in has impacted my heart for gathering.

There's a reason God impressed the importance of showing love to strangers throughout the Old Testament. We see it found in Leviticus 19 when God commanded Moses to tell the Israelites the following:

> When an alien resides with you in your land, you must not oppress him. You will regard the alien who resides with you as the native-born among you. You are to love him as yourself, for you were aliens in the land of Egypt; I am the LORD your God.
>
> **LEVITICUS 19:33-34**

Write these verses in your own words.

The Israelites were intimately acquainted with what it felt like to be strangers, foreigners, and hostages of their hosts. Chained and grappled by the bondage of Egypt, they understood freedom and God's merciful rescue. And when they didn't have a home, God provided food and shelter as the Hebrew people wandered in the wilderness (Ex. 16–17).

God wanted the Israelites to remember their own desperate loneliness, their struggles, and their years in slavery, so they could empathize and create a safe space for others who needed to be welcomed, because they knew and would understood in ways that others couldn't.

> For the people of God in the Old Testament the duty of hospitality came right from the center of who God was. I am the Lord your God who made a home for you and brought you there with all my might and all my soul. Therefore, you shall love the stranger as yourself. You shall be holy as I am holy (Leviticus 19:1). Your values shall mirror my values.[2]

That's the cornerstone of why hospitality matters so much. It matters to the heart of God. Not only was it foundational to His nature but also to the theology of hospitality. This heart of the gospel that's rooted in a gift of invitation weaves its way throughout all of Scripture, and we've only touched the surface. When we welcome and invite others into community, it's because we're driven by one overarching principle: love God, love His will, and point others to His glory.

Since we've started at the very beginning, let's remember why we are here. Prior to our salvation, we too were strangers, foreigners, orphans to God, and separated because of our sin. Yet because of His hospitality extended to each of us, we are strangers no more.

> So then you are no longer foreigners and strangers, but fellow citizens with the saints, and members of God's household, built on the foundation of the apostles and prophets, with Christ Jesus himself as the cornerstone. In him the whole building, being put together, grows into a holy temple in the Lord. In him you are also being built together for God's dwelling in the Spirit.
> **EPHESIANS 2:19-22**

Paul reminded us that it's about sharing our lives.

> Because we loved you so much, we were delighted to share with you not only the gospel of God but our lives as well.
> **1 THESSALONIANS 2:8, NIV**

One of the easiest ways to show love is to invite others into community with us: to practice hospitality.